C000186590

The GREATEST
in the WORLD

illustrated by
Peter Bellingham

Linda Jones

The Greatest
Freelance
Writing
Tips in the World

A 'The Greatest in the World' book

www.thegreatestintheworld.com

Illustrations:
Peter Bellingham
www.peterbellinghamillustration.co.uk

Cover & layout design:
the designcouch
www.designcouch.co.uk

Cover images:
© Jon Helgason; © Csaba Peterdi; © Hazel Proudlove;
© Gaja Snover; © Mateusz Zagorski
all courtesy of www.fotolia.com

Copy editor:
Bronwyn Robertson
www.theartsva.com

Series creator/editor:
Steve Brookes

Published in 2007 by
The Greatest in the World Ltd., PO Box 3182
Stratford-upon-Avon, Warwickshire CV37 7XW

Text and illustrations copyright © 2007 – The Greatest in the World Ltd.

A CIP catalogue record for this book is available from the British Library
ISBN 978-1-905151-17-2

Printed and bound in China by 1010 Printing International Ltd.

For Neil, Emily & Melissa.

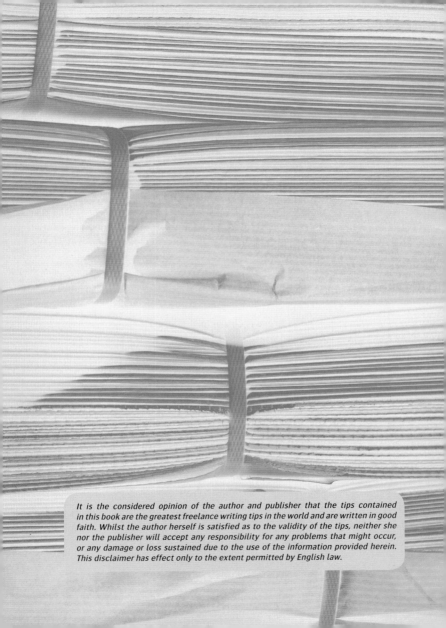

Contents

A few words from Linda …

Writing is a tough old business – and I love it. Over the last three years I've built a company out of my freelance writing career and consider myself very lucky and privileged to make a living out of something that I enjoy so much.

But that's not to say it has been easy. Anyone who goes into freelancing thinking the streets are paved with gold needs to get a grip. Times are tough for many freelancers – so make sure you are going in with your eyes wide open.

The best way to get ahead in freelancing is to start by looking for a part-time job. Yes really. It is very unlikely (but not impossible) that you can make a good living straight away with no experience in publishing or the media. You need to build up contacts and establish a reputation. Unfortunately neither of these pays the bills.

This book is designed for those at the start of a freelance writing career, but might also be of help to those who have already made some progress.

My aim was to offer realistic advice, as far too often what I've read on the subject has been nonsense. It's not a complete step-by-step guide to bring you freelancing success. Nor is it a 'How to write' guide. I'm clinging on to a belief that anyone wanting to make a living from writing might already have an inkling of how to do that!

Instead it's simply a collection of tips, observations and pointers amassed over 16 years in journalism, the last eight of them as a freelance, the last two as a blogger – a testimony of a jobbing journalist!

So who am I to be offering this advice? You read about some of my professional background in my 'About the Author' section. The company I started, Passionate Media, was founded in 2003. My fellow director, Carol Garrington, has since been named 'UK's Most Exceptional Working Mum' by **www.motheratwork. co.uk**. There are five of us altogether at Passionate Media — all working a variety of different hours. We have been featured in research by the British Chambers of Commerce on flexible working and have been praised by the CIPD for 'leading by example'.

My colleague Katie is one of the best writers I know. Her background? As a supervisor at a magistrates' court, she had few opportunities to hone her writing skills. Bringing up sons Ben and Alex doesn't leave much time for journalistic success.

But over the last year or so Katie has written for The Daily Express, Take a Break, Real People, Love It and more. She is a wonderful example of someone with a passion and natural talent for writing and a strong work ethic — and that's why she's succeeded. I'm so very proud to be working with her and Carol and they are an inspiration every day.

I hope you enjoy these tips collected together as one of the Greatest In The World series. A perfectly modest title, I'm sure you'll agree. Why The Greatest? Well I can honestly say these are hints and tips that have worked for me, and you can't say fairer than that, now, can you?

Happy reading and writing.

Foreword

When I tell people I'm a freelance writer, they are usually pretty impressed. Some even admit to being a little envious. Hardly surprising, as most people assume I live a charmed existence; getting up late, sitting around watching daytime TV, idling away hours in cafes, sipping cappuccino and waiting for the muse to strike.

There are many myths about freelance writing. The first is that it's an easy ride. While there are many advantages to the freelance life (flexible hours, no boss to answer to, and the freedom to choose when and how you work, for starters) it is very hard work. Not only do you have to do the work, you also have to find it! It's is a crowded market, so most editors can afford to pick and choose, meaning freelance writers are always under pressure to find fresh, interesting story ideas that stand head and shoulders above the rest.

Writing is also just a small part of the equation. Being a competent, accurate writer is a prerequisite for a writing career but writing ability alone won't pay the bills. Ideas are currency. If you can't come up with story ideas that editors want on their pages, and pick up the phone and sell your ideas, you might as well forget it! There is no room for big egos in freelance writing. Editors are busy people; they can be hard to pin down and cautious about using new writers. Even the most successful freelance writers hear the word 'no' far more than 'yes'.

There are many books and magazines out there that cover the topic of freelance writing but they are often written by amateurs who have yet to land a feature or undertake a commercial copywriting contract. As a result, the advice is often outdated and inaccurate. What's different about this book is that it is written by someone with hands-on experience. As a former regional news editor and contributor to various print and online publications, Linda Jones knows what editors want. With nearly 20 years of journalism experience behind her she knows exactly what makes a good story and what will get editors eating out of her hand. She also knows how to land commercial writing jobs that get her clients coming back for more.

She knows how to deal with tricky editors, argue the toss over rates and copyright, how to handle rejection after rejection – and so much more. She knows because she's been there. She's got the book, the album, and the t-shirt. If I'd had this book when I started my writing career, I would have saved myself a lot of time and money!

I have no doubt this book will become a must-read resource for freelance writers who have all levels of experience. It's a no-nonsense book which tells you like it is. Writing can be the greatest job in the world and these could possibly be the greatest tips!

Good luck!

Jan Murray

Jan Murray is a freelance journalist writing for various broadsheet newspapers, largely on education, and Editorial Director of the thriving JournoBiz resource website for media professionals, www.journobiz.com.

The role of a writer
is not to say what we
all can say, but what
we are unable to say.

Anaïs Nin

Getting started

chapter 1
Getting started

FIRST THINGS FIRST

Writing as a business

Remember at all times that if you are serious about making a living from freelance writing then you have to take it seriously. You think I'm stating the obvious, don't you? I'm not, I promise; I have encountered too many wannabe writers over the years who reckon they can rake in the riches by sending out articles and hoping for the best. If you are going to work for yourself, then guess what, you're setting up a business. Get all the advice you can on that, and if it all sounds a bit scary, then it's not for you!

Writing as a hobby

I wish you good luck with your hobby. Enjoy it, nurture it, take pride in it, notch up every success by shouting your achievement from the rooftops, but please don't make the mistake of thinking everyone will take you seriously. Beware of the editors you might find "ferocious". Research your target markets well (more on this later) and be prepared for a rocky road.

Reality check

Think about what you are expecting from your writing endeavours – if you are anticipating editors calling you offering exciting assignments for pots of money within weeks of starting out, then you need to come down off your cloud and decide how you can really make a go of things. Set targets for what you would like to achieve month by month, whether that's alongside your current full-time or part-time job, or to make your hobby fly, and do all you can to reach those realistic goals.

Ask yourself:
What sort of work can I be confident of finding?

Think you're going to be jetting off to a film première to interview the stars or test-driving the latest Mercedes because you fancy giving it a go? Sounds good to me! But seriously, why would anyone in charge of such top jobs give them to anyone without proven experience? The reality of freelancing as a career for many is a constant whirl of mundane jobs, chasing payment and seeking new opportunities. So why do they do it? Well, in my case anyway, when those opportunities come off, it can be fantastic. I'm an optimist – you can make it as a freelance, but I'm a realist too. As one esteemed colleague used to tell me: "You can't expect the moon on a stick."

Ask yourself:
And why will YOU make it exactly?

For me, this is the key question. What can you offer editors that the millions of other aspiring or successful writers haven't tried already? Be honest with yourself. If you can't answer this question, then it might be time to move on. Writing for fun is one thing, but if all you are going to do is end up floundering because your ideas are the same as everyone else's, what's the point in clinging on to false hope?

I don't think I'm being unduly harsh here. Even the most established freelancers with decades of experience in the media behind them have so-called dry spells – otherwise known as the 'feast and famine' of freelance life. Take a long hard look at your experience, knowledge, and skills, and don't kid yourself about how much you're going to starve!

Organisation, organisation, organisation

We've all heard the clichés about us "creative types" being a nightmare when it comes to paperwork, filing, and other admin stuff, haven't we? Well wouldn't you agree that these things often become clichés because they are rooted in truth? I am the world's worst record keeper (believe me, it's true) but these days I find myself surrounded by spreadsheets, job sheets, contact lists and update charts! How sad is that? But seriously you have to find a way of keeping track of your efforts, including work done, pitches sent, money owing, and ideas for future projects.

Time is of the essence

So when are you going to write then? Think you can just fit it in with all the rest of the demands of your busy day? Who's going to do all the other stuff you have to do, if you lock yourself away in your back bedroom with nothing but your computer for company? (I'm writing this from my back bedroom, by the way, the house is a tip. My partner is downstairs and so are three eight year-olds. I'd better get a move on as I have to cook a chicken.) But, it is vital to plan your time. Are you a morning or evening person? Can you burn the midnight oil? Do you really have to watch the latest instalment of your favourite quiz show when you could be knocking out 500 words instead? Be ruthless, declutter your day.

Working for yourself

Are you unemployable? I know I am. I have already listed some key attributes of freelance writers on page 48, but before you take the leap, here are some other factors that could determine your success:

- You couldn't work for anyone else now.
- You have the support of those around you.
- You come from a family of people who have set up their own businesses.

BUSINESS PLAN BASICS

Write down your:

- Targets.
- Budgets.
- Projections.
- Timescales for achieving.
- Plan your marketing.

Include:

- Who will buy your work.
- How you're going to reach them and when.
- Incomings and outgoings.
- Where you will work. Focus on every detail of how you believe your freelance writing business will work.

Working from home

Ask yourself:

- Am I being realistic?
- Can I earn enough for this to be my sole income?
- Can I organise my work well enough?
- Can I burn the midnight oil to earn enough?
- Am I self-motivated enough or will the lure of daytime TV be too strong?
- Will I feel lonely?

Some basic points to remember if you have young children:

- Don't expect to be able to work while they sleep or play around you.
- This especially applies to making phone calls – I have learned from bitter experience.
- Make child care arrangements just as if you were going out to work.
- Organise your day so that your get quality time with your family – not sit at your computer when you could be reading a bedtime story, if you would really rather be doing that.
- Consider finding a shared office space with other writers. If you have to conduct interviews then where can you do this? Expecting your contacts to step over Barbies with no heads on or Buzz Lightyear toys might be a bit much!

Get to grips with grammar

"Don't worry about spelling, just tell the story!" Every time I hear of someone dishing out this advice, I want to gnash my teeth and bang my head on the table.

It might be sound guidance if you are in a room with other would-be storytellers working on a joint project for fun, but if you ever present an editor with a piece of work where the apostrophes are nowhere to be seen, or you have written 'there' for 'their' (I've seen worse) then you can bank on not writing for them again. Make Lynne Truss the best mate you ever had. (If you don't know what on earth I'm talking about, hey, why not look it up?).

Get to grips with copyright

You will retain copyright of your work unless you sell the licence to reproduce it to a publisher outright, so a copyright sign isn't needed.

Placing the copyright symbol © with your name and the date/year of when something was written is usually sufficient to protect your material.

If you want extra peace of mind that your work is safe from being copied you can undertake some additional measures. You may add a legal phrase at the bottom of a page (print or web) saying something like "This work is the property of the author and may not be used or reproduced under any circumstances." There are many examples of so-called copyright terms on the web. You may alter the wording to suit your preference. You can find other phrases in use if you look at various websites or other resources (see Additional Reading if you are looking for inspiration).

But, and it's a big but, I really wouldn't go down the "extra protection" route. If you have an exclusive interview with Madonna on the adoption of a child or a piece shedding light on an explosive political scandal, then maybe this is justified. But as a beginner, I'd say you're more likely to annoy the people you're writing for than impress them. I have a copyright sign on the homepage of my Got Your Hands Full website, but can't remember ever using it elsewhere.

Get to grips with libel and contempt

If you are mouthing: "What's that then?" then you need a reality check! There's not an editor in the land who'll publish your work if it contains a legal howler. Get yourself a copy of the most recent *McNae's Essential Law for Journalists* and make sure you understand what on earth it's talking about. Some might protest it's not needed in today's ever-changing writing world. Well they're wrong.

Newspapers and magazines can call on their legal teams to check whether anything that is deliberately provocative is "safe", but as a writer, you don't have that luxury. Don't ruin your reputation as a "safe pair of hands" before you've even got off the ground. Find out about media law and stay well within it.

In the dark about pitches?

If I had a fiver for every time I'd seen a discussion about people sending their articles off to magazines (possibly even handwritten) then I'd be a very rich woman indeed. There are times when writing 'on spec' might be called for, but please, as you start on a path to freelance writing, don't be under any misapprehension that this is in anyway the norm. Editors want to see ideas, or 'pitches' and these need to be as tightly and professionally presented as possible. More on this in Chapter 3.

Ask yourself: Can I trust this advice?

Every aspiring writer knows there's a world of resources to tap into, to help chase their elusive dream of hitting the big time but beware, please don't jump head first into buying a course off the Internet. Take all promises of freelance wealth with a pinch of salt. There are freelance writers who earn six-figure sums, I know there are, but for every one of these, there are ten struggling hacks waiting to find out where their next commission will be coming from.

Find out all you can about any tutor or training site first. Who are they? What have they written? How often have they been published? Where can you read their work, and why are they tutoring? Ask them for testimonials from former pupils willing to put their full name to fulsome praise about their inspiration. I once shelled out for an online course about 'Writing for the Internet'. When I saw much of it was about writing for free, I asked for my money back.

Aim high, start low

Never miss an opportunity when you're starting out, even if the pay isn't great and the work isn't something you'd want to do forever. You never know what something might lead on to or how much work might come out of it. Any clip is useful in the early days. But having said that, be wary of all 'writing for free' opportunities. See Chapter 2 for more on this.

Finding markets

Aha! Another key element of successful freelancing and another one that seems to attract hogwash masquerading as advice. "Buy a writers' handbook", say some, "Get your hands on Media Disk", say others, "type *writers wanted* into Google and see what that brings you". These are all examples of some of the ways it's often suggested that you can find places to sell your work. And yes, they can help. But again you must beware: books and disks go out of date very quickly, the 'writers wanted' positions are snapped up very quickly and might pay peanuts. I like to equate the worth of the job to whether or not those seeking help know what an apostrophe is. Too often you'll see all manner of things said to belong to writers but there's not a correct use of the 'possessive' in sight!

So what else can you do? Now here's a thought: it's pretty basic if you ask me. Study the publications you want to write for, find out if they are open to freelancers, whether they pay, and how much, and if you still want to, send them a pitch they can't say 'no' to. How difficult can that be? Oh okay it's pretty difficult, but I do hope that reading this book might help you.

Don't take rejection personally

Well, unless you've just been kicked to the kerb after 20 years of marriage of course. There's not a working freelance writer who doesn't hear the word 'no' more than 'yes', I can tell you.

Just this week I emailed four ideas to a section editor on a national newspaper. He came back and said that he "really wasn't interested" in the first, "couldn't care less" about the second, and declined to comment on the third. Luckily for me, he said the fourth sounded "interesting" so I've hounded, sorry, kept in touch, with him and filed 1,100 words since then. Another idea on a separate theme was also accepted a couple of days later.

Imagine all the ideas these people receive. Why on earth should they come back to you at all? They never asked you to get in touch! And if you do get a curt "no", pick yourself up and have another go. If on the other hand, you get: "It's not quite there for us, but do keep trying", then a dance around the room may be in order, not to mention dazzling them with another finely-tuned pitch that screams: "use me, use me".

Quick tip

WRITER'S BLOCK? FORGET IT!

Don't give me that excuse! Yes sometimes we all stare at the blank page and wonder why the little voice in our head is telling us we'll never fill it. Tell the little voice to take a running jump, and get on with it. How many words do you have to write and when by? How much are you being paid? And how much was that electricity bill again? Does that help? It sure helps me.

DID YOU KNOW?

To err is human
Joseph Priestley discovered the rubber eraser in 1770, using pieces of rubber imported from Brazil. Then in 1858, Hyman Lipman of Philadelphia, Pa., patented the pencil with an eraser at the end.

Editors, huh?
Can't live with 'em, can't live without 'em

Newsflash: editors are okay. They are human, they love their children. They might even have done their time as a freelance. Wahay! If you are scared of editors, then don't be! (Go on, admit it, some people are; hard to believe, I know.) Treat them with professional courtesy and respect, and you should be okay. Reply to their queries, meet their deadlines, get their names right and don't let them down — what more could they ask?

But also remember, they need to do the same to you. I'm whispering now but some editors can be a tiny bit vague. They'll give you an unclear brief and expect you to calibrate your crystal ball to tune in to what they want. Some might even be — wait for it — difficult to please. They might ask for more and more until frankly, you're losing the will to live.

I'll leave it up to you as to what you might want to do about working for them again.

And what about the writing?

As I said in my introduction, this is not a guide on how to write. You should find a much better means of finding that out, before you have the brass neck to approach an editor to ask if they'd like to publish your work.

But I'll say this: keep it simple. Why use 50 words, when you can use 10? Why use five syllables when you can use two? Clear concise copy is what counts, not how much irreverence, or how many clever words you can use per line. My training told me that if someone had to read your intro twice to understand it, you've failed miserably. It sounds obvious, but how often can we say the stuff we read every day fulfils that oh-so-simple requirement?

Check your facts – then check again

The title says it all. Research skills are vital. Make sure your references are sound. Just because something has already been published online or in print, doesn't make it true. If someone is quoted as having an opinion, then contact them direct to check. Use your conversation to go in different directions to make your article even more interesting.

Remember: A deadline isn't an optional extra test!

It's cardinal sin time. Repeat after me: "I will not miss my deadline, I will not miss my deadline, I will not miss my deadline". Okay that's enough, you get the picture. If you know in advance, through no fault of your own, that you might miss your deadline then negotiate an extension. Otherwise not only do you look like an idiot, you might not get work from that editor again. And what a shame that would be, especially when there are about 50 other would-be writers waiting to step into your shoes and who are perfectly capable of delivering on time.

Quick tip

WHERE ELSE CAN YOU FIND WRITING JOBS?
1. *Media Guardian*
2. *Press Gazette*
3. **www.freelancersintheuk.co.uk**
4. **www.writersmarket.com**
5. **www.freelancers.net**
6. Recruitment websites – **Fish4jobs.com** etc – writing jobs can and do appear

Chapter summary:
Getting started

As you start out:

- Be businesslike.
- Understand copyright, contempt, and libel.
- Manage your expectations: be realistic.
- Get organised, plan when you can write.
- Ask yourself: what's so good about me?
- Learn not to take rejection personally.
- Forget writing articles then trying to sell them. Learn the art of the perfect pitch.
- Don't miss deadlines.

> It is impossible to discourage the real writers – they don't give a damn what you say, they're going to write.

Sinclair Lewos

The business of freelancing

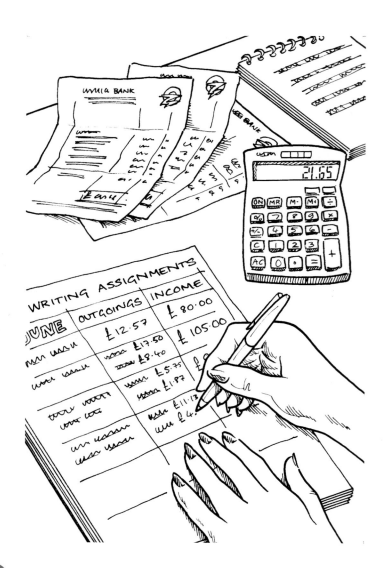

chapter 2
The business of freelancing

Ask yourself:
Can I afford to go freelance?

Plenty of people don't, you know. Shocking isn't it? How could anyone be so stupid? In my view, the simple answer is 'yes', as long as you are confident of enough work to pay the bills.

Tot up your monthly outgoings on the mortgage, bills, food and other essentials. If you have the contacts, experience and drive, not to mention work lined up to match or exceed this total, then go for it. But still proceed with caution. Even the most successful freelancers might have a rocky start.

In my first month as a freelancer, I earned £160. The next, a little more. For the next 12 months, feast and famine set in, with earnings some months at around £7,000, but mostly at £1,500–£2,500. And some months I didn't crack £1,000.

I'm in the lucky position of having a partner on a modest wage and also had the small matter of two young children to look after – that's why I could afford to go freelance – because we took the attitude that whatever I earned amid looking after the kids was a "bonus" and we were prepared to make sacrifices.

If you think you are going to rake in the cash weeks into a freelance career, then think again. We got by because entertaining two little girls doesn't cost much. "Feeding the ducks is free", I'd say as we set off for the park, and it also happens to be a great inspiration for flogging some features.

Quick tip

A TAXING MATTER

Go and see your local tax office before you file your first piece to make sure you are doing everything right. Look into tax and national insurance. I am not a tax inspector nor am I an accountant, but I can tell you that if you put off doing this, then you could be sorry. (I was, thanks to a £100 fine for not sorting it soon enough.) Resources for the right advice when setting up a new business are at the back of this book.

Show me the money: Ask yourself, should I write for free?

Would you expect a plumber or mechanic to do their job for free? No? So why do publishers instruct aspiring journalists to submit their finely crafted features without any pay? Ask any new writers and they'll tell you how difficult it is to 'crack' that elusive vicious circle: you want a job, editors want experience. You pitch a feature; they want evidence of a track record – cuttings of already published work.

So what can you do? Writing for free is a harmless way of proving you have what it takes, isn't it? Well no, actually. You must beware – for every publication offering you exposure as your sole reward, there are plenty more experienced hacks who'll tell you to tread carefully.

Writers should be paid a fair wage and those who routinely work for free are effectively undercutting those of us who depend on writing for our livelihood. Do you see?

Are you being ripped off?

- Ask yourself "Is this publication ripping me off or do they genuinely have a limited budget?" If so, why? If they can't afford to pay their writers, why is this, and do you really want to write for them?

- Weigh up if the piece will genuinely have the possibility of leading to other work, building a specialism or boosting your reputation.

- Be prepared to ask for a fee if a job is going to take a lot of work. Ask for expenses at the very least.

- Do you care passionately about an issue you are reporting on? Will it make a genuine difference? (And even then some would say "remember, the resulting warm glow doesn't pay the bills".)

More on rights and copyright

"Help, an editor has stolen my idea!" Noooooo. Stop right there. What a coincidence – your idea about a calendar for crafts activities has been nicked by a major publishing house. What nonsense! You can guarantee that the day Victoria Beckham gives a nod to her latest thoughts on health or family, there'll be plenty of writers – staff and freelance – who'll be attempting to sell a piece on 'ordinary' women with the same concerns. Except of course, they'll call it a 'case study'.

Read this and remember it, pin it up on your fridge (or your computer monitor might be a better idea, sorry) if you like: *There is no copyright on an idea.*

If you do happen to spot a feature in a magazine or newspaper that you reckon looks 'similar' to something you suggested, then either congratulate yourself on having the right sorts of thought processes or have a word with yourself about being too obvious. But don't spend a minute stressing over what might have been.

Who says they weren't already working on the piece before you came along? Who says another freelance didn't suggest the same idea, someone who already has an 'in' with the editor?

Of course there are exceptions to every rule, but that's my story and I'm sticking to it. And no, I'm not saying that because I've nicked anyone's ideas!

There's a great guide – *10 Things Every Freelance Should Know About Copyright* – available through the National Union of Journalists.

Contracts: Read the small print

When you are commissioned to write a piece for a newspaper, magazine, or website, you should be asked to sign a contract or agree to the terms of the job. You must check the small print carefully. Some places will be happy to take work on a "second rights" basis, others will insist on "first rights", while an increasing number are expecting you to pass over "all rights", something the National Union of Journalists has something to say about! This is from the NUJ: "What you sell to an editor is a license to use your work, once, in one territory, in one medium. Examples are First British Serial Rights and World Wide Web Reprint Rights."

In every case, read the contract carefully. Otherwise it will come as a shock to you when your carefully crafted prose pops up in another magazine or newspaper – without an extra penny coming your way. Raise any queries with the editor or seek advice about how you might be able to challenge the "rights grab".

I love writing.
I love the swirl and
swing of words as
they tangle with
human emotions.

James Michener

Please Sir, can I have some more?

"Ooh, I'm so rubbish at asking for more pay." "Eeek, how can I get more money, I don't want to tick off my editor."

If ever either of these sentiments begins to figure in your way of thinking, then it's time to take action. You can ask and sometimes you will get more money. Believe in yourself and your abilities, but don't ask for trouble.

For example, some newspapers will tell you what their rates are. Even then you can treat them as the minimum payment to expect, so there is no harm in a polite enquiry as to whether they can be improved. If you have turned a piece around under exceptional circumstances, such as getting hold of someone who would never usually speak to the media, or you have stepped in after another writer has let the editor down, then rates could be negotiable.

Whatever the fee, make sure you know it when you accept the commission. That way, nobody can pull the wool over your eyes (as if they would!) and you know where you stand.

Within reason, you can always negotiate. What have you got to lose? No editor worth their salt is going to think you are pushy if you do so, so long as you are in a position of strength, and in my humble opinion, that means you have a brilliant story and you supply great copy.

What do I mean by "within reason"? Well I wouldn't fancy your chances much if you asked for more money after you've already accepted the fee offered, have been picked up on any grammatical mistakes in your pitch, or don't have a single cutting to your name, just yet.

Sometimes a client will ask you what you will charge. When this happens, I ask them what budget is available, or I name a price based on various factors — how major is the publication, how good is the story, how much work will it take? And possibly the most important, how big is the PITA factor? That's Pain in the A*** if anyone is wondering.

The NUJ run Pitch and Deal courses which are open to members and non-members alike. Why not give one a go? They also publish an excellent Rate for the Job guide, but again, they stress, these fees can be treated as the minimum.

How to set the rate for commercial writing jobs

The dos and don'ts of commercial writing are covered in Chapter 7, but for now, let's ponder the thorny issue of how to set a scale of charges for a commercial client.

They might ask you to write, sub, proofread, or edit their newsletters, other marketing material, website or press releases. They might ask you to do more stuff on top, like sending out the press releases, liaising with journalists, or getting their cuttings together.

So, are you going to charge per word, per page, per hour, or per project? Phew that's quite a list, and I've seen various answers over the years. My answer? It depends. Oh dear, sounds a bit of a cop-out. It's not, I promise. For most people it comes down to a choice of per word or per hour. There are pros and cons to each approach:

Per word pros:

- You know where you stand.
- If the work can be done quickly, it will be lucrative.

Per word cons:

- This doesn't take into account the time taken. What if you have to chase for amendments approval and wait for them to come back? What if they ask you to change wording you think is actually okay?

- If it takes you an age to complete through no fault of your own, then you can't do much about it. At least negotiate a rate for working on amendments if/when the client changes their mind.

Per hour pros:

- Billing for your time means you can more accurately forecast your earnings and know how much time you have left for other work.

- If the work is additional marketing or administrative duties on top of the writing then it makes sense.

Per hour cons:

- Clients might view this option with suspicion.

- You might have to include an hourly breakdown to show what you have been spending your time doing.

If the work doesn't take you long then you might have been better charging per word.

What else do you need to take into consideration? When setting a rate, you really need to focus on what it costs you to work. What are your overheads and how much do you have to charge to cover them? Ask yourself if you are prepared to offer different rates in different circumstances, depending on whether this is an ongoing project or one-off job.

Or look at the client's circumstances and decide can you, or should you, do them some sort of deal? Ultimately, that's your decision and nobody else's. But allow me to offer one tiny word of caution: don't get too caught up in offering deals, discounts, or even freebies in the hope that someone will come back for more. Guess what, they might not.

Whatever rate you decide on, always, always get an order form/contract signed up front. It's harsh but true that you cannot afford to do anything on trust. Some characters, unfortunately, will do anything to get out of paying. Establish stringent terms and conditions.

Chasing payment

Start at the beginning. Get in touch with the accounts department of the publication that has accepted your article and ask them how they pay. What information do they need on the invoice to process it quickly? Find out the name of the person you'll need to speak to in accounts, plus their direct line and email address.

Accounts departments like the easy alternative and if your invoice has all the relevant information on it, the more likely you are to get paid on time. So that means:

- Name.
- Address.
- Phone Number.
- Email details.
- Date.
- Work completed, number of words, for which edition.
- Your own reference number or code.

- Any purchase order information or reference number assigned by the commissioning editor.
- Terms and Conditions of payment.

Ask when they need your invoice by to ensure the most prompt payment.

If the expected payment date comes and goes, and no money appears, ring your named contact and ask when you can expect the payment. If days turn into weeks, send a statement and ring or email as often as you can. Please don't hold back on this – that's your money they're holding on to. And what's more you can charge interest if the client hasn't paid up according to your terms. Speak to Business Link or check out their website for the latest information on that.

A killer blow: Don't accept a smaller fee if your piece doesn't appear

My heart sinks just thinking about it. For all those papers that 'over-commission' there are dozens of writers chasing payment on pieces that never saw the light of day. If you met your brief, you should be paid in full. End of. But of course it's not like that – find out a publication's policy on 'kill fees' before you write for them. If you don't like it, you might want to reconsider.

If you haven't met your brief then you might have to accept a kill fee but not before they've given you a chance to get it right.

chapter summary:
The business of freelancing

Remember:

- Make sure you can afford to go freelance.
- Sort out your tax affairs.
- Develop a healthy cynicism towards writing for free.
- Negotiate confidently.
- View kill fees with suspicion.

Everything in life
is writable about if
you have the outgoing
guts to do it, and
the imagination to
improvise. The worst
enemy to creativity
is self-doubt.

Sylvia Plath

Writing for newspapers & magazines

chapter 3
Writing for newspapers and magazines

No news = bad news

If you have a story you don't think can wait then pick up that phone, tell the newsdesk and follow instructions – they might want you to follow up on it, or they might ask a staff writer to take the details. Either way you can pocket a cheque and for the time it's taken to make a phone call, that can be more than worth your while, so long as you don't put the phone down without settling on your fee.

Your local paper might not have the budget to reward you handsomely, but what about the nationals? Read the tabloids – what sort of news stories are they featuring and could you give it a shot? Personally I wouldn't get into the 'kiss and tell' shenanigans – but what about the quirky, off-the-wall stories that raise a smile? They all have to come from someone. Why shouldn't it be you? Keep your ear to the ground in your local community and who knows what you might discover!

Hit that target

When pitching features, you could have the best idea in the world, but if it's sent to the wrong place, it will stand what's technically known as a snowball-in-hell's chance.

Get to know the sections you want to take a shot at. Are their pages filled with bylines from staffers or are they open to freelancers? What regular slots are there and are they on a theme or in a style you are confident you could match?

How do you know if you'll hit the spot? Research, research, and research again. Start small with 'fillers' and letters — they can pay a small amount and shouldn't take up too much time.

Writing on spec: It's not always big and it's always not clever

First of all, please may I say this: there are exceptions to every rule. Some publications might welcome 'on spec', unsolicited, fully researched and written articles, so please do not write to me to tell me that *Leek Growers' Weekly* once published your fascinating article about pest control.

But by far the best idea, when targeting ANY publication, is to get in touch with an idea to gain the editor's interest, allowing them to advise how many words they want and in which direction they would like you to take it.

If you have already laboured over a completed piece, you have wasted your time.

Having said that, if you do contact some more esteemed publications (*The Times* and *Times Educational Supplement* spring to mind) then as a new writer, you might be asked to write your piece on spec, to see if you meet the required standard. What do you do then? Some people waver but my advice is go for it!

Make your pitches work for you

Want to know how to guarantee an editor comes back to you with a "Yes please, that sounds great!"? Hey, don't we all. I can't offer a magic solution to that conundrum, but I can tell you how to give your pitch the best chance possible.

And if you're wondering what on earth a pitch is, then you need to wake up and smell the coffee. Forget labouring over a 1,000 article to send off to a new editor. What's the point of that? They might love the idea but want you to take it in a wholly different direction. And they're the boss.

So here's what you do. I've been asked for a template in the past so I hope this helps:

Don't forget to include all contact details – home, work, mobile, the lot. You won't be very popular if they can't get hold of you to commission your long-laboured-over gem of an idea.

- **In the subject field:** Attention-grabbing title relevant to the publication you are pitching.

- **In the message:** Dear (name of editor)
  Re: Attention-grabbing title relevant to the publication you are pitching.

- **Then**: One to three paragraphs explaining what you would like to write about. Be as succinct as possible. If you are suggesting more than one idea, then number them and space them out well.

- **Then**: Thank you for your time, I'll welcome any feedback.

- **Then**: A paragraph headed: 'About me'. Explain why you are the right person to write this piece, listing relevant experience and links to any published work.

Here's a real life example:

- **Subject field**: Who you looking at? Dumb things people say to twins/parents of twins.
- **Message**:

  Dear Jane,

  Re: Who you looking at? Dumb things people say to twins/parents of twins.

  I'm a freelance journalist specialising in writing about multiple births and I wondered if you'd be interested in the following. I'd include interviews with mums about the daft things they've had said to them and include my own experience as a parent of twin girls.

- **Intro**: "Double trouble eh? You've got your hands full!" Just a few harmless words from an interested well-wisher to a mum or dad of twins, right? Wrong! These two short phrases can strike terror into the heart of any parent of multiples, and make even the most mild-mannered of mums want to lash out. Yes I know they are only meant in a kindly, inquiring sort of way – it's just we've heard them a million times before.

  But like Richard Wilson when another besotted fan quotes Victor Meldrew's "I Don't Believe it!" catchphrase to his face, we smile and nod like it's the first time we have ever heard such a witty remark …

- **About me**: I'm a former journalist with the *Express & Star* and mum of baby twins. I'm now seeking regular freelance commissions to help me find work as my girls get older.

Now then – I hope that "About me" bit helps – it was the fact that I'm a mum of twins that swung it, I'm sure. Of course mentioning I'm a journalist is going to help, but the pitch was good enough to win the editor over without listing a load of published articles on parenting.

Here's how my pitches have been able to evolve. This is one from a few years later, accepted by *My Child* magazine:

- **Subject field**: Telling off other people's kids
- **Message**:

  Dear Helen,
  Re: Telling off other people's kids
- **Intro**: According to parenting experts, it's a common dilemma. Families have different tolerance levels and varying approaches to discipline, but are fearful of making an issue of it in case it causes a row with the other parents, or can feel awkward applying their 'rules' to someone else's family. What do you do when little Chloë is trying your patience when you've invited her for tea? This would include a case study of a mum who 'didn't want to rock the boat' and one who says: "I don't think twice about telling them off. If they are with me, they have to behave!" Plus hints from an expert on how to find the option that's best for you.
- **About me**: I've written extensively on parenting for a number of publications including the *Independent on Sunday*, the *Birmingham Post & Mail*, *Express & Star*, **www.babyworld.co.uk** and *Tamba's Twins, Triplets & More* magazine, of which I was editor.

Six of the best
vital attributes of a freelance writer

1   **Strong work ethic ...**
Forget the fantasy of swanning around in your dressing gown, penning your oeuvre when the muse takes you. Right here's where you start paying – in sweat! (And okay, possibly in your dressing gown.)

2   **In-built bull**** detector ...**
Don't go anywhere without it.

3   **Tenacity ...**
Try hard, then try harder. Never give up.

4   **Courage ...**
Freelancing favours the brave.

5   **Willingness to market yourself ...**
You can't hide your light under a bushel – shout from the rooftops about your experience and skill.

6   **Writing talent ...**
Yes it does matter – but possibly not as much as you think!

Not many cuttings so far? Don't despair!

A lawyer might be considered to be in a better position to pitch an article about a miscarriage of justice than a more dispassionate and established writer, so long as their pitch is well presented, concise, and engaging. It all depends on the style of article and how expert the writer is. In this particular example, some editors might question partiality, but most often 'insider knowledge' can be a definite plus.

Your life experience might be much more attractive to an editor than a clutch of cuttings from someone without your passion. Just don't let that passion run away with you in your pitch.

Where to send your pitch

I've browsed many a website looking for 'contacts' at different publications – what a waste of time that was! Despite the advice from the "amateur scribes" online (their words, not mine!) who give a postal address and tell you to send a hard copy in a brown envelope, written out in pen, your best bet is to get the exact name and direct phone number and email address of the section editor you are targeting.

How do you do that then?

Well you could ring the paper or magazine. Yes really. If this scares the pants off you, listen very carefully, I shall say this only once: you might not be cut out for freelancing. It involves, like, talking to people. Or (even more shocking) you could buy the publication and look on any list of staff included to select your prey, sorry, contact. There might also be an editorial assistant you could contact but beware this might be the busiest person on the features desk, so don't always expect a warm welcome.

Should you send your pitches by phone or email?

Here I go again: it depends. Editors are so busy now that they won't take kindly to you ringing right on deadline to pitch an idea, however good it is. Nor will they welcome a zillionth email chasing them over an idea you first sent just three days ago.

So what can you do? Finding out when they are least likely to be busy, for a start. Yes it's their job to look at freelance pitches (possibly) but please don't moan if they don't reply. I've said it before and I'll say it again — they didn't ask you to contact them, so why should they race to reply?

I send most pitches by email. This gives the features or section editor time to digest it at their own pace. Some come back straight away. "Thanks for thinking of us, but it's not quite right. Good luck placing it elsewhere", says one editor, without fail, sometimes in the blink of an eye. How does she do that?

A colleague on another section of the newspaper says: "Thanks but I'll pass on this one." This usually takes him a day or so.

Some come back and say "Yes please, X words ASAP" or words to that effect. I like it when a plan comes together!

And others never reply.

It's the editors in this last group who can cause the most anxiety for any freelancer.

That's why it pays not to leave it to chance. If you have real confidence in your idea, there's no harm in sending another email a little while later (say a week or two) asking for feedback, as politely as you can muster.

On one memorable day, I did this three times and clinched three commissions.

After that, you might like to phone. People seem to hate doing this. I used to be incredibly shy in all sorts of ways so I can understand this, but if the choice is don't ring and not get the work or ring and find out the editor loves the idea but couldn't reply earlier due to covering for a colleague. Now which would you prefer? The £250+ in the bank, I'd hope.

There is a time and place for everything and sometimes, even before or instead of emailing, you've got to pick up that phone. And when might that be? Well when the story's a cracker! That's when.

Examples? This is where the hugely-competitive but very financially rewarding human interest or so-called real life stories can come into their own.

Over the last year, examples of stories I have placed include one about a woman who had triplets after a series of heart-breaking setbacks, another about a girl who was kept off school because bullies made her hair fall out, and a third about a woman who had a visit from the police over a missing shuttlecock.

My 'bravery' as some would have it, was rewarded with six immediate commissions, as I sold each story twice.

Make your heading work for you

What do I mean by attention-grabbing?

Here are three of my headings that worked:

- Mummy, that lady has a beard! (*Take a Break*)
- My Boxing Day hangover was triplets (*Pick Me Up*)
- I conceived twins in twin hurricanes (*Take a Break*)

And here are three that didn't:

- Diary of a Virtual Assistant (Boring!)
- Can marriages be saved by counselling?
  (What was I thinking?)
- From midwife to ghosthunter (Hmm, quite liked that one!)

The 'so what?' test

Think about what is so different about your idea. Why is it current now? And why are you the one to write it? A general piece on 'home education' might not be deemed worth looking at, and could easily be researched and written in-house. But a piece on home education with a cracking interview with a mum who refuses to send her son to school because of bullies, might be nearer the mark – especially if there has been a topical or newsworthy development on a national scale.

Watch the time!

How many times have I read that Awareness Weeks make great hooks for stories? Yawn. Too many. Beware. You can bet that if you know next month is Bowel Cancer Awareness Month, so will many other wannabe contributors. Again, what's so very new and different about your angle?

Lead-in times for publications vary. Pitch a monthly with a Christmas story in October, and you are marking yourself out as a fool. Phone and find out when the deadlines for copy are.

Building a specialism

Put yourself ahead of the competition by honing in on one of your passions. Sign up to research documents, specialist publications and even foreign journals relating to your chosen field. Get to know of, and keep in touch with, experts in the same field, keep track of new developments and innovations and show editors how on-the-ball you are. Keep a blog detailing latest news in the subject area, seeking and responding to comments from other interested parties. Attend conferences, meetings or trade shows, and get to know what and/or who is hot or not!

Ideas are everywhere

Turn every experience into the potential inspiration for a feature. From family activities to your views on reality TV, there is a possible market to be found. Take your notepad everywhere – ideas can crop up in the strangest of places.

Read your favoured publications regularly. What topics are they covering and how could you contribute?

Sign up to news alerts from Google, read the BBC online, check out sites that distribute press releases relating to the subjects that you are interested in. These are all fine examples of ways to keep up to date with what's happening in the world, or certain parts of it. But also, don't forget about people. Find interesting characters in your area with intriguing or inspirational tales to tell and help them tell their stories. Study all the specialist or weekly magazines you can to predict realistically where your pitch could find a home.

Let talking to people be the backbone of your research. An enthusiastic, charismatic or inspirational human being will help you with food for thought far more than any printed document.

Kerching! Real Life stories

What sorts of subjects are needed for a successful real life pitch? That's a pitch to the hugely popular women's weekly magazines. For a start, I'd say anything that has happened in real life but this begs the question "can it really have done?" Tales with a happy ending are good sellers, so long as they are the sort of happy ending the readers can empathise with or dream of.

Examples from my real life portfolio include:

- I married the best man.
- Five generations of love.
- Walking tall: I'm so proud of you sister.

So where do you find such stories? Again it's a matter of getting out and meeting people, putting the word around that you are looking for stories and what sort of stories you're looking for.

Six of the best

myths about freelance writing

1 It will make you rich – and quickly ...
Excuse me while I stop laughing. Newsflash: you're
not going to get paid on time, every time. Get used
to this prospect but determine to do all you can to
stop it happening.

**2 Writing an article in full before sending it to an
editor is always a good idea ...**
No. This isn't right. The pitch is the thing.

3 Editors are all ogres ...
They're not.

**4 Your writing talent is the single, most important
factor in your success ...**
It isn't. The ability to find stuff to write about, to elicit
the right information and to chase for payment, should
all be jostling for position at the top of the list too.

5 It has to be an isolated pursuit ...
Oh no. You can embrace all sorts of opportunities
online to make new contacts and friends. Don't think
you have to be lonely.

6 Research is easy ...
Please don't fall into the trap of thinking that checking
stuff out starts and ends with Google. Talk to people,
consult other resources, make sure you can trust the
information. And as my journalism trainer used to say:
"If in doubt, leave it out!"

Personally, I wouldn't advise taking stories from local papers or small news websites as there might be other freelancers or agencies chasing the same stories. Beat the competition by finding your own.

Get to know the ladies in your local hairdresser, laundrette or corner shop. Take time to chat and see what crops up!

Step-by-step: A women's magazine feature

Breaking into the highly paid so-called real life market can seem daunting for a number of reasons. The nature of the stories covered isn't for everyone, and the level of personal details needed can prove off-putting for those who don't fancy asking such potentially difficult questions.

Here's my step-by-step breakdown of what happens next:

1. There should be no pressure and no offence if the subjects of the story change their mind. These are personal stories and you can't go ahead without their permission.

2. If they have already been featured in a mass market publication, then you won't be able to place their story.

3. Use brief information to put together a pitch to the magazine. Ask them for a picture from a family album, scan it in and send with your pitch, or get a jpeg. Supply the basic details that a magazine will want. These are: the ages of everyone in the family, full names, full address and dates of birth (those last two not for publication) and occupations of all members of the family.

4. Send your pitch and selection of pictures to the editor to give him/her an idea of the person whose story you are telling. If this is your first foray into this sort of market then

send it to one editor at a time. If you are more confident that it's a great tale, it might be worth your while trying several at once and plumping for the best offer.

5. The editor would come back saying whether he or she wanted the story and if so, what fee would be paid to both you and your interviewee – who might be referred to as your "case study".

6. He or she would send you a contract which the case study signs promising not to talk to other media until after publication.

7. Once you have submitted your story, which you should write according to the publication's guidelines, it might also be added to by a staff writer. Do not be disheartened, unless they do a full rewrite and ask a load more questions! You have done your job so long as you have provided compelling, legally sound copy which answers all the questions the magazine's readers might have.

Look after your contacts: It's nice to be nice!

Journalism is one of the most cut-throat and cynical professions you're ever likely to encounter.

To listen to some reporters speak, you'd think they've hated every minute. The miserable old so-and-sos do nothing but moan about declining standards and how it was all so much better in some mythical golden age. My answer? Get a life! It's nice to be nice.

When I worked in my first reporting job, my colleagues used to rib me about how sympathetic I was to people who rang in with a possible story. Sometimes the caller wanted to moan about the damp in a council flat, sometimes they wanted to tell us about their parents' Golden Wedding, or even a lost dog. Some were lonely and appreciated a chat with a daft young woman on their local paper, even if it was to advise that we were banned from writing about missing pets.

As soon as I put the phone down, the laughing would start. "You're not a social worker", my colleagues would chip in. But it's funny, those same people would ring back, again and again. Sometimes it would be to say they had some interesting background information about a current court case, or that they knew someone who'd just had their 13th child, or was at the centre of an important investigation.

So it was the young "social worker" (as opposed to the reporter who barked to the council tenant about her damp "Yes and how do you think I am supposed to help you?") who found her name more frequently on the front page or her stories in the nationals the next day. I remained in touch with some of these people for years and they became the sources of some more cracking stories or ideas.

So what's the point of sharing this here? Well I think it's good to remember that you never really know who you might be talking to when you first hear from them. Treat your contacts well and they will help your writing career flourish. Poor 'people skills' can mean professional and financial suicide. Not only do you need to build relationships with people and organisations in your areas of interest (often from scratch), you need to cherish those contacts. And why not cherish the editors too? Now there's a thought.

chapter summary:
Writing for newspapers & magazines

Remember:

- Be a newshound.
- Target feature pitches well.
- Avoid writing on spec.
- Watch those 'lead in' times.
- Don't write off women's magazines.
- Keep your eyes open and your ears to the ground.
- Cherish and nurture your contacts.

> Being an author
> is like being in charge
> of your own personal
> insane asylum.

Graycie Harmon

Interview &
research skills

chapter 4

chapter 4
Interview & research skills

Elsewhere in this book, you'll see that to make it in freelance writing, the writing is just one of the things you have to worry about – and that there's no room for shyness. The understanding of these two aspects comes together most closely when you are doing an interview.

There's no such thing as a stupid question.

Think you don't know enough about a given subject to write well about it? Nonsense! Reporting skills mean you can research the subject and ask the questions that matter to a mainstream audience.

For example, if you are writing about technology, the article is likely to focus on what the technology allows you to do, rather than the ins and outs of the technology itself.

On my training course all those years ago, I was told "there's no such thing as a stupid question." I still agree. As the interviewer, I'm not trying to dazzle the interviewee with my knowledge of the subject; I'm representing the readers who'll hopefully enjoy my piece later, asking the stuff they will want to know.

And how can you do that? Put yourselves in their place: they might not know what all this jargon means and they aren't as close to the subject as you are. If you don't understand an answer, nor will the readers, so take great care to make sure what you're writing is clear enough for everyone to understand.

How to manage it?

Telephone, face-to-face or by email? The best interviews are done face-to-face, so that you can observe your subject's body language as they respond to your questions. You can see how they fit in with, and relate to, their surroundings, you can put them at ease more, learn more about their life from what they choose to surround themselves with, and take in the atmosphere! You can also challenge them and react more naturally to their responses, by taking the conversation in any direction that fits, however unexpected, but still making for a better story.

In the early days of the relationship, face-to-face interviews can also help you, as well as your subject, gain confidence and there's no better way to hone your interview skills.

But these aren't always possible and these days you are just as likely to find yourself chatting, quizzing, or grilling over the phone, as you are knocking on someone's front door.

Telephone interviews

Prepare questions that you must ask, but allow the conversation to develop as if you were face-to-face. There's no point sticking to your keenly crafted questions when your subject reveals a nugget of information that will take your story to a whole new level. Take a deep breath and ask them about what they just said. Go with it and you'll be onto a winner.

Email interviews

I hate these but I still use them, sparingly. Sometimes an interviewee will request an interview by email, or if you are going to be speaking to them, they'll request sight of the questions in advance. Treat such requests with suspicion. Why on earth would someone want to do that? Put yourself in their shoes: perhaps they are overly nervous and have never met a real life writer before. Do all you can to put their mind at rest and assure them there is nothing to worry about. I'd politely decline the request to see the questions in advance, unless there were exceptional circumstances – and by that I mean George Michael giving me a private audience! Move over Parky, your time is up.

There is a huge problem with email interviews. Although the interviewee can favour them, all spontaneity can be lost. You can't see their reactions, you can't jump in with another follow up question and you won't have a clue what your subject makes of your interview. It's also incredibly frustrating when a carefully thought-out question comes back with a simple 'yes' or 'no' – so please do avoid email interviews unless you really, really can't. At the very least, ring up your subject and talk their answers through.

Record your interviews

In 16 years of journalism, I have twice been asked to produce a shorthand note of a conversation I've had. Both times, despite complaints about being "misquoted" by the interviewee, the editor has been happy with the accuracy of my notes.

I'm an old fashioned sort and I would very much like to recommend that anyone considering being serious about a freelance writing career learn shorthand. But I know that's not going to happen.

But you still need to record your interview and there are a host of funky (and not so funky) devices on the market to help you do this.

Do take notes too. My memory of a health conference in Birmingham circa 1999 isn't great and nor was it by the time

I came around to writing about it as the deadline approached a couple of weeks later (not an approach I'd recommend!). Thank goodness for my pages and pages of notes when my first and only attempt at using a Dictaphone failed spectacularly. The Dictaphone worked all right – there was just far too much background noise for me to make head or tail of what the speakers were saying.

So how do you start?

Take time to make your interviewee feel comfortable. I do this by explaining once again who the piece is for, when it's likely to be published, how many words I'm writing, and what angle I'm hoping to take. You can, of course, choose to chat about the weather instead. It really doesn't matter in my opinion, so long as you put them at their ease, instead of launching in sounding like a grand inquisitor as opposed to someone wanting to help tell their story.

Back to basics

I remember being interviewed as a mum who was willing to speak about healthy eating for children. Glossing over the fact we were in a Kentucky Fried Chicken at time, the journalist (Lucy Jolin) said to me first off, confidently but gently "Let's get the basics out of the way first", before proceeding to ask me if she could check the spelling of my name, where I lived, how old I was, what I did for a living, what my partner does and how old the kids are. Phew! I was really impressed – up until then I'd always left this 'belt and braces' information until the end of an interview but these days would heartily recommend Lucy's approach.

Six of the best

markets that accept approaches from freelance writers

1   **Filler slots in women's magazines ...**
Check out the letters pages of all the most popular weekly reads - amusing snapshots and family anecdotes are the order of the day.

2   **Filler slots in some sections of the Guardian ...**
Which ones? Do your homework and don't send anything before checking.

3   **Shiny Media (www.shinymedia.com) ...**
Lots of blogs on lots of subjects. Aspiring writers welcomed.

4   **The Guardian blogs (including Comment is Free) ...**
Go for it if you can — but only if you are prepared to have your work pulled apart in the sometimes pretty vicious comments section.

5   **Local glossy county magazines ...**
Like other slots mentioned on this list, they might not be the best payers but an interesting local story can look great in an early portfolio.

6   **Specialist publications ...**
Here's where writing what you know can hit the spot. Impress the editors of titles serving a sector you have experience in with your well-targeted and timely ideas.

Go on – talk!

Ask open questions – not ones that can be batted off with a simple 'yes' or 'no'. Don't make your questions over-complicated; help the conversation flow. If you get an inkling that your subject isn't comfortable, take a moment to find out why this is. Then you can decide whether to make them feel more at ease or plough on regardless. (Sometimes it'll be your job to nudge them into telling you things they might not want to give away!)

Again, if you really don't feel right about asking awkward questions, please consider whether this is the right path for you. You are far more likely to have your copy thrown back at you because it's full of holes where you should have asked more questions, than being told the writing isn't right. Sub-editors can tinker with copy to make it fit better or tidy it up – they might view that as their job; but they won't be best pleased if you have missed out basic or key information.

Quick tip

PUT YOUR HANDS UP

And when your editor asks you a question about your subject that you haven't sought to answer, don't reply "She didn't say." I hate that with a passion. Far better to admit, "I didn't ask, sorry." Yes, you might consider it a little embarrassing but you can be sure to remember it next time.

The answer's "no", now what's the question?

Can interviewees see your copy before you forward it to your editor? "No" is the usual answer, as it's just not accepted practice and you have an accurate note of what they said, and when. You should remain fair and impartial at all times, and that includes not being swayed by interviewees into letting them influence how you are going to report their story or quotes.

An exception to every rule

The most obvious time you can show your interviewee what you have written is when? Well when they are paying you to write about them, whether it's for a press release, brochure, advertorials or other marketing material. They are the client after all, so it's no good getting on your high horse!

The other time that I might read my copy to its subject is when the story is a very sensitive one. I want the interviewee to feel comfortable and confident at all times that I can be trusted, and may need to check the facts through again if it involves serious illness or bereavement, for example.

Where to find your interviewees

Clue: it's not always online.

Click onto any forum for writers and you might find an abundance of "case study requests". There are even websites dedicated to helping people star in the media, putting them in touch with journalists keen to tell their stories.

Proceed with caution. But really, where on earth can you start? And why should you even want to help? Would aspiring estate agents or lawyers expect established rivals to offer up their contacts?

"When a man is in doubt about this or that in his writing, it will often guide him if he asks himself how it will tell a hundred years hence.

Samuel Butler

In my days of being a miserable so-and-so on a newsdesk I know I wouldn't have been impressed with such blatant attempts to crib off other people, expecting to be handed information on a plate.

Now, it seems for many of us, me included, pressures on our time through home, work, and family can mean we reach out for the quickest solution.

But there's still a danger isn't there? How exactly do you know that the contacts you make through the Internet are any good? Who are all the other members and how useful is their advice?

People can mean well but do they really know what they are talking about? And what if they are like the audience on the Russian version of Who Wants to be a Millionaire? They deliberately misled some poor soul when he chose to ask them for their help, didn't they? You do find some mischievous blighters on any forum.

DID YOU KNOW?

Hear ye!

The urge to inform the public of official developments and pronouncements has been a characteristic of most autocratic rulers. This urge was fulfilled in ancient Rome by the first recognised 'newspaper', the Acta Diurna ("Daily Events"), a daily gazette dating from 59 BC and attributed in origin to Julius Caesar. Handwritten copies of this early journal were posted in prominent places in Rome and in the provinces with the clear intention of feeding the populace official information.

Is your "case study" right for your target publication?

This is what's technically known as a right can of worms. Increasingly, it seems that the women you interview won't make the magazine you are pitching at, because they don't look right, whatever their story. It's a topsy turvy world we live in, that's for sure.

But if you are going to pitch a feature that concerns one or more women, do take the time to find out whether they are of the right age group and social group to be considered for inclusion in a particular magazine.

Ask many a staff or freelance writer and they can quote you chapter and verse on women's glossies rejecting case studies or even whole features because of what the subjects look like.

In general, they'll say they want 'smart, modern, thinking women'. Sadly that means your interviewee might not be quite right but she could be for someone else.

Writers have learned how to play the game although it doesn't always feel right. It's up to you if you want to. There is plenty of money to be made from the magazines who don't insist their featured women should be "photogenic", and, to be fair, they often have the best stories.

DID YOU KNOW?

Tap, tap, tap!

The first practical typewriter was invented by Christopher Latham Sholes, and was marketed by the Remington Arms company in the year of 1873.

---

chapter summary:
Interview & research skills

Remember:

- Face to face interviews are best.
- Ask all the questions you know will need answering – even the 'stupid' ones.
- Make your interviewees feel at ease, if possible.
- If not, plough on regardless.
- Always take notes: don't rely solely on recording equipment.
- Be careful about case studies.

> When something can
> be read without effort,
> great effort has gone
> into its writing.

Enrique Jardiel Poncela

Writing for the Internet

chapter 5
Writing for the Internet

Although many people seem to think the Internet is to blame for the decline of newspapers and journalism (though of course ignoring readers' wishes might be a bit higher up the list) it still offers a wealth of opportunities, especially for freelancers.

The biggest growth area in writing in recent times, online publications are now rivalling 'dead wood' media as sources of news, information, and entertainment. That means there are plenty of opportunities for new media-savvy writers, with plenty more to come. But beware – plenty will want you to write for exposure (nothing!) or for a pittance. Have a look back at Chapter Two and check if that's really for you.

Keep up with the times

Websites, and in particular those from news organisations, are likely to include not only text and pictures, but also possibly video, audio, graphics, and animation.

Also, don't forget that an increasing number of people are no longer relying on a static page on their computer screens to bring them their news and features. They might be accessing it via a mobile phone, a personal organiser, an RSS feed, or a digital TV screen.

And when they do access that information, don't sit back and expect them to have nothing to say about it. You are likely to be writing something for a truly interactive site, so brace yourself for some lively feedback and think about how you are going to respond.

Be willing to evolve as time goes on, but don't ever think you can afford to ignore the basic principles of providing sound, engaging copy, on time.

K.I.S.S – Keep it simple, stupid!

Why use 50 words, when you can use 10? Why use five syllables when you can use two? Keep it simple! Don't make the mistake that just because your writing is on the Internet that you need to get down with 'da yoof'. Clear concise copy is what counts, not how much irreverence per line.

You should be concise, direct, and relevant, hitting your reader with the most important points at the top of the page.

But as with newspapers and magazines, what you should know is what's relevant to your target audience and what the house style is.

Hook your readers – and don't let them go

Internet readers are more likely to scan or skim articles, so ensure your copy is going to keep their attention as well as can be expected. Expect to use sub-headings, bullet points, 'pull out' quotes, 'boxouts' or 'fact boxes' as per the editor's directions. And if you don't understand any of the terms used – then ask! (A boxout is of course, a box out of the usual text, with some extra information included in it.)

Don't assume your readers are experts

Help them understand: explain any specialist terms, don't use big words to show off your knowledge, and don't make the mistake of trying to cram in too much jargon. Make your writing as accessible as possible – that's a good way of writing whatever your medium, but especially so on the Internet.

KNOW YOUR AUDIENCE
Who is the site for? How many people read it, of the 500+ million people with access to the Internet? What do they need to know and why is what you are writing important to them? Don't assume anything, find out!

Stick to the style guide

You may write "per cent" in other articles, or form the date in a certain way. It'll be different and more concise online.

Most websites have a style guide. Treat it with the respect it deserves. Stick to the font and the way of presenting copy that's spelled out. If there isn't one, then do ask the editor for pointers. They might surprise you with a contributors' guide.

Online research – be careful

People can hide behind a computer keyboard to make up all sorts of stuff, as some pretty nasty court cases have shown in recent years. Check the details and then check again. If you find a possible interviewee via the Internet, do all you can to make sure they are who they say they are. And if you read something that could be worth a mention in a piece you are working on, then make sure you can 'stand it up' by more traditional means, say, by digging out the details of anyone concerned and checking directly with them.

I'd rather be caught holding up a bank than stealing so much as a two-word phrase from another writer.

Jack Smith

Six of the best

websites to add to your writing knowledge or experience

1   **www.writersfm.com**
Internet radio station with interviews and tips for aspiring writers.

2   **www.responsesource.com**
Brings together journalists looking for a story and PR people wanting to supply them with one that features their client.

3   **www.trashionista.com**
Brilliant site which made me an avid reader, again.

4   **www.motheratwork.co.uk**
Fantastic resource and support for women juggling home-life, career and children, who don't want to drop too many balls.

5   **www.wikipedia.org**
Huge online, free encyclopaedia but double check all information if you can.

6   **www.imdb.com**
Check out the work histories of actors, directors and other film talent.

Join the blogosphere

Understand what a blog is — that's an easy-to-update website. Although the 'easy' bit is important the key element is 'update'.

Get one for yourself. They are free through **www.blogger.com** or **www.wordpress.com** and cost a few pounds a month through **www.typepad.com**.

Not only can a blog showcase your writing, it can also help you develop your style for writing for more online markets.

In the past people found it difficult to update their website as it usually involved asking another company to place the new text on the site and often a fee was charged.

Not surprisingly websites quickly become static entities with very little information beyond contact details, an overview of the business, and a list of services.

But the Internet never stands still, and although this type of site might have been suitable in the past, search engines now look to highlight websites that offer fresh articles and are talked about on other sites.

The old five or six page static websites are sadly lacking these key elements.

However, blogging software allows you to easily update your site, automatically sets up links to new articles on your site, enables readers to ask questions and tells both search engines and followers of your writing that you have written something new.

Banish your preconceptions about blogs

No they really aren't just places for teenagers to talk about school and for others to argue politics.

Well sometimes they are of course. But if you look a little further up the assembly line of these types of sites then you will see that whether people are complaining about cross-country class or the state of the Health Service, they are just publishing articles on the Internet.

For years people have published their thoughts and ponderings via pamphlets, newspapers, and brochures. Today this process has been taken onto the Internet so basically everyone is using similar tools. They are just publishing different words to different people.

Nothing has really changed: it has just become easier to do and possible for an individual to attract a worldwide audience.

A freelance writer can use the same tools as the teenager or the politico.

Understand how you can benefit from a blog

Before I go any further it is important to stress that you will only enjoy success with a blog if you are willing to give time to writing articles.

I can't stress enough the importance of that. If you think you will enter something new on the site once or twice a month a blog is not suitable for you.

With that out of the way just some of the benefits include:

Your website will establish you amongst your peers as a person who follows your subject, provides an online resource where both your own experience and that of others can be found, and allows interested readers to follow your writing. This establishes you as a commentator in your sector and so you gain strong benefits and presence elsewhere.

Another key benefit is that you are pre-qualifying visitors to your site, as many will arrive at your website via a search engine. People often turn to search engines with a question in their

Six of the best
writing blogs

1 **www.buzzmachine.com**
US journalism professor Jeff Jarvis on all things new media. Keep up to date with the latest thinking on how 'old media' is being overtaken by the new.

2 **www.gettingink.typepad.com**
Sally Whittle on all things PR. Read about how PRs influence journalists — with some notable foul-ups.

3 **www.problogger.net**
Darren Rowse on how to make money on your very own site.

4 **www.bbc.co.uk/blogs/theeditors**
Read about the issues behind the scenes at the BBC.

5 **http://tojou.blogspot.com/**
Teaching online journalism
Does what it says on the tin.

6 **www.wordblog.co.uk**
UK journalism lecturer Adam-Grant Adamson on how the media landscape is changing.

minds and it is the job of the likes of Google, Yahoo! and MSN to find an answer.

Because your site is often updated, has clean and simple links to your articles and is easy for search engines to find, then, if your site provides an answer, you will feature on the results page.

So already that person has seen something that might well answer their questions. When they read your article, or find other pieces that highlight something they had not thought of, and your blog gives them the option to post a question there and then, there is a good chance you will have developed quite a link with this person.

The comments being left by people are also a benefit because they will point to problems and questions that visitors have, and so provide you with an insight into a need. Consider it free market research for article ideas.

Clinch that book deal or TV gig!

Yes really! A blog can unlock a great deal of potential. Publishers scour the Internet for unsigned writers with an original voice, people who can entertain and inform, provoke debate and build a loyal following. There are several bloggers who have hit the literary heights and there's no reason you can't join their ranks.

Or promote your blog's niche interest by establishing yourself as an authority on your chosen subject. I've been contacted by four (count 'em) national publications wanting to chat about twins and more thanks to my 'Hands Full' blog. Every little helps!

So what are the key features of a blog?

Beyond the fact that they are often updated there are some important aspects of a blog that are the same, or very similar, regardless of which software or service you use.

One of the most important elements is Permalinks, which, although a bit of a cumbersome word, basically means that each of your articles has its own address on the Internet.

This is important because think of the number of times you have put a page into your favourites folder to read a little later and when you head back it is no longer there and you can't find it anywhere on this site.

Permalinks ensure your article never moves: it sits there so that others can link to it from their own websites, forward in an email, or just write down and pass to a friend. So when this person decides to follow up this recommendation your article is there for them to read. You never know — they might tell another friend.

Naturally your writing might cover different subjects within a wider subject so it would help if you could ensure this partition exists on your blog as well. This is possible through the use of Categories, which allows you to put different articles under different headings. A visitor can find everything you have written about a particular subject and cut out those articles that don't interest them.

Archive your writing by date

So, your blog software will automatically generate a Permalink for your latest piece, place it in your chosen category, put a date stamp on it, and file it under that month or week automatically.

Another key element is that all these links within your site allow both readers and search engines to find your articles, because the first thing people ask about a website is "will anyone read it?" and "can search engines find it?"

Well there is no better way to achieve this than make all the internal links containing descriptive text point to your writing. Should something appeal to a reader they can click a link and start reading, or a search engine can read the link and get a pointer to what the resultant page is about, and so add to its knowledge of your site.

It also means that others can link to you and help promote your site as readers of the original site will trust the author's recommendation and click through. Search engines will also move from the site to yours and measure the importance of that link.

If someone comments – comment back!

With these people now on your site you want to try to ensure that they feel part of it and let them interact with it in some way. The ability to leave Comments on a blog site is another feature that makes them stand out from regular websites, but is the feature that most worries people.

Thanks to your blogging software, each article can have a Comments feature at its foot so that people can add their own thoughts, leave useful advice for other readers or ask you to clarify something.

Comments on your site show that it is an ever evolving spot on the Internet and it can soon build up to provide tightly focussed information on individual articles. They are also very helpful for search engines.

Some of the most popular blogs are those with busy Comments sections that are continually generating snippets of text on a particular subject.

As a small aside, some of the biggest websites on the Internet are those that allow users to create the pages for them. If you think about eBay, people actually pay to update the site! So if you let people leave comments, your site is receiving new text without you actually writing anything.

However, as I mentioned a little earlier, the Comments facility on a blog is the bit that worries people, because what if someone writes something stupid on the site?

Again, your blogging software will allow you to moderate any comments being left by people so that you can cast an eye over them to see what they say before allowing them through on to your site. But a word of caution – don't use this moderation facility to ignore questions posted by disgruntled readers.

Remember, search engines register as many websites as they can and look for useful articles to help answer questions. So if someone posts a complaint through the Comment facility and you fail to act on it, they could easily write about their problems with you on their own website, going so far as to detail all the steps they took to try and sort them out.

Their writing would feature your name and so search engines would be able to register this. Should someone cross this site, then it is a poor reflection on you, and all because you failed to act upon one comment.

You can turn negative comments around to ensure any damage is kept to a minimum and even show you acted swiftly to ease your reader's worries. One way would be to publish their comment and then directly beneath write a reply saying what you will do.

The other is to write a new article about the person's complaint, indicating what you did to help them out, and how you have changed things within your business to try to make sure something similar doesn't occur. After all we are all human and make occasional mistakes. Showing people how you have dealt with a situation is a great reflection on you.

Finally with all these new articles going on your blog you want to be able to tell readers when there is something for them to read, without relying upon them to remember to visit or pop your site in their 'favourites' folder.

Again, blogging software will have the facility to publish something called an RSS feed, which is a way for your website to tell other computers on the Internet that you have something new for it to check.

If a reader of your site is interested in following what you write they can ask their feed-reader to check your site's RSS feed and tell them when a new article is published. So when you next post a piece your new site visitor will get a message in their reader, and with one click they can be reading your latest article.

The style guide begins at home

If you are looking to make your website work hard for you and boost your business then it needs to look professional.

Not only should you study style guides carefully, you should also adhere to one on any website or blog to showcase your writing.

The design and style is something that you most probably take a lot of time over, but what about the words themselves? It is important that your articles look as one, that readers are not confused by the appearance of the words on the screen and that your audience is comfortable reading what you write.

"If you want to get rich from writing, write the sort of thing that's read by persons who move their lips when they're reading to themselves.

Don Marquis

chapter summary:
Writing for the internet

Remember:

- Keep it simple.
- Keep up with the times.
- Check your style.
- Get blogging.

"You write to communicate to the hearts and minds of others what's burning inside you. And we edit to let the fire show through the smoke."

Arthur Polotnik

Other writing

chapter 6
Other writing

Are you the next Maeve Binchy, John le Carré or Marian Keyes? Possibly. Give yourself the best shot by allowing time to write, developing your talents, and finely honing your craft.

That means you might not get to write your great novel just yet. A more sensible approach is to start with short stories and exercises. Get to know your strengths and weaknesses and take it from there.

Find your own voice

You may love Maeve, John, or Marion, but well, you're not one of them are you? So do your best to find your own voice – and that doesn't mean inventing a plucky hero or heroine with your initials and having them follow a path similar to your own.

Be original, be daring, write from the heart, and edit with your head.

Find some friends

Forget all that stuff about solitude breeding creativity: join a writers' group (online or in the flesh) for feedback on your work and to gain mutual support. But be prepared for everyone to be far too nice. Visit your local reference library to find details of your nearest group or check in the listings in one of the publications for writers.

Six of the best

basic tools for a start in freelance writing

1 **Order newspapers and publications covering your favourite subjects ...**

You must keep on top of what's happening in the world ... and that means every 'world' you write about. Studying foreign titles (say US or Australian) might also help you find ideas to pitch.

2 **Computer equipment: word processor and internet/email connection ...**

Don't think you can wing it. Get expert advice and make sure everything is set up as it should be.

3 **Notebooks dated and filed as you progress ...**

Don't think you can get away with a succession of scraps of paper covered in hastily scribbled notes. Believe it or not, this has been a very basic but difficult lesson for me to master. That interview you have just done, you might just need to look at it again.

4 **Contacts database ...**

List and order your contacts – somewhere you can easily find them. It sounds obvious, it isn't. Those interviewees you've just chatted to – you might just need to speak to them again.

5 Systems in place: work and ideas in progress and accounts ...

Goodness that sounds complicated. It needn't be. Set up a system to suit you. Include date of pitch, deadline, completion date, all names and contacts of editors/accounts people, and anything else you want to add, then away you go.

6 Invoice template

Believe it or not, I've been contacted by writers asking how to prepare an invoice ... after they've done the work. If you don't know what you are going to put then you aren't in a position to do the work. Do you need a reference number or purchase order for a specific job, or do you need an invoice at all? You'll look like an amateur if you leave finding out these nuggets until after you've done the work. So start as you mean to go on ... and get it sorted.

Short stories for women's magazines

As a new writer, particularly one with a journalistic bent, this market could be your best bet. These are publications you might already be familiar with, and have an inkling as to what their readers will enjoy.

Get the style right

Your story needs to flow, and have pace, punch, and flair. Forget all the flowery stuff — you haven't got the space.

With this in mind, contract everything, i.e. he'd, she'd, we'll, I've, you've, they've — you get the picture.

Plot matters: know your audience

Make sure your story is something the readers can relate to and your heroine one they'll take a shine to. Make her surroundings and situation familiar to the readers — help them laugh with her, or feel for her.

Avoid the following hackneyed plots like the plague. They've all been done at least a million times before:

- Animals (especially cats) telling the story:
  oh what a surprise!

- Identical twins swapping identities to play a trick:
  goodness I never saw that coming.

- The blind date or dating agency 'match' being the husband:
  you'll never top what's gone before.

Instead, think of contemporary, everyday situations the readers can identify with.

My freelance colleague Kelly Rose Bradford, who has had stories published in various magazines, lists the following as favoured scenarios. But remember, each needs a fresh 'take':

- Marital disputes.
- Teenage tantrums.
- Spouses taking each other for granted.
- A new arrival (could be a baby, or a pet, or even a foster child).
- Battles of the sexes.
- Sibling rivalry.
- Holidays from hell.
- Families at war.
- Looking for love.
- Betrayal.

DID YOU KNOW?

2B or not 2B?

The word pencil is derived from a diminutive of Latin peniculus, "brush" – which itself is actually a diminutive of penis "tail". Chaucer also holds the distinction of having first used the word pencil (c 1386) as the instrument used in painting. By 1612, a pencil was a writing instrument – a thin cylinder with a tapering point made of various materials such as chalk, charcoal, graphite, plumbago, slate, etc. The amount of clay used determines the degree of hardness of the lead in a pencil, e.g. No.1 is soft, No. 2 is medium-soft, etc.

The devil's in the detail

Forget those fancy fonts. Stick with Times New Roman or Arial and adhere to guidelines on how to submit your work. For fiction at least, this usually still means good, old fashioned double spacing, no right hand justification, new paragraph for each new speaker, no extra lines between paragraphs, and numbered pages. A cover with the name of the story, plus all your details, should also be attached.

Some examples of magazines taking stories, and what they want:

Bella – 1,000 words, no first-person stories.

Best – 1,000 words.

Candis – 2,000 words.

My Weekly – 1,000–4,000 words.

People's Friend – 1,000–4,000 words plus serials.

Take a Break – 1,000 words.

Take a Break Fiction Feast – 1,000+ words.

That's Life – 1,000 words.

The Lady – up to 2,000 words.

The Weekly News (newspaper) – up to 1,500 words.

Woman – 1,000 words.

Woman's Own – 1,000 words.

Woman's Weekly – 1,000 & 2,000 words plus serials.

Non-fiction books

There is a huge market for non-fiction books and if you have developed and nurtured a specialism, then there's no reason why you shouldn't give it a go. Get to know specialist publishers in your field and present them with a synopsis in the same way you would send a pitch to a newspaper or magazine editor.

Alternatively approach an agent and discuss your ideas. The agent can call on their experience and guide you in the right direction.

Just as you wouldn't prepare a full article for an unknown editor, you don't have to complete your book before gauging interest. Research how to best write a synopsis and prepare to dazzle. Oh, and have three chapters written ready to show what you can do!

How to present a synopsis

Make it as compelling as possible — just like a pitch. If you are sending a pitch on-spec by email to an agent (and you should do this one by one rather than sending it out to lots at once) then, as well as stressing the depth and skill of the writing, you should also plug how you can help shift copies of the book.

Here's the format of a synopsis that gained me concrete interest from a publisher. (Yes okay, I'll admit the project fell through in the end, but I'm still assured the pitch was excellent, thank you very much!)

Subject: Publishing enquiry: 'Iconic image' of xxxxxxxxx speaks out

Dear

Please find to follow a synopsis for a book that is under way. I am the ghostwriter. We have not approached any other agents or publishers. Should you feel it worthwhile representing us, we would be keen to maximise marketing opportunities by working with you to complete the book as soon as possible.

I appreciate that timing is crucial. I have put this synopsis together at a very early stage in the hope of getting things moving. Because my background is in a senior position with daily newspapers, working to tight deadlines, you can be assured of a fast turnaround, should that be required.

I would welcome your feedback at the earliest opportunity.

SYNOPSIS: MY STORY BY Xxxxxxx (Working title: I'm just Joe Public)

Examples of some headlines about the case

CONCEPT

Xxxxxx offers a unique insight into the events of xxxxx. He was at the heart of the events of the biggest UK news story of xxxxx and came to symbolise a country's defiance.

Xxxxx can explain what it's like to be at the centre of the sort of international media clamour that is usually reserved for world leaders, bringing him fleeting instant fame. He has been invited to Washington and New York to meet VIPs and has rubbed shoulders with statesmen and celebrities.

Xxxxx is determined to tell his own story. He has read the wise words of columnists and media pundits who were distanced from what happened and he would like to provide a lasting record of the voice of an ordinary man – albeit one whose face was published on hundreds of newspapers worldwide.

Most importantly, he says, he wants to reinforce the message that the 'force for good' represented by ordinary people going about their everyday business cannot be beaten by murderous fanatics.

CONTENT (includes)

1. The fateful day.

2. The ensuing media coverage and Xxx's experience of being at the centre of it.

3. How his life has changed.

4. Revelations that Xxx's role wasn't the first or last time he has been called a hero.

5. Hopes and fears for the future.

- Author profile: include relevant credentials and full details of any previous books (title, publisher, date, sales figures).

- Competing books: list the main similar and/or competing books and analyse how yours is different/better.

- Market for the book: who will read it and why. List both general and specific readerships: international general, UK general, and specific.

- Promotional possibilities: include anything you can do to publicise and market the book (the more you can do, the more the publisher will do).

- International, national, specialist, and regional coverage.

- Length and scope: the number of words and illustrations.

- Images.

- Delivery: how much is already written and when you will have a finished manuscript.

- List chapters.

- Avoid self-publishing if you can help it.

- Self-publishing is the last resort. Get your book published and distributed at someone else's risk and expense. Don't think that if you go down the self-publishing route everyone will take your work seriously.

Six of the best

online resources

1   **www.journalism.co.uk**
Features, news, jobs, freelance directory and more —
an indispensable resource.

2   **www.journobiz.com**
Excellent 'how to' articles, plus 'featured journalists'
and one of the most supportive forums.

3   **www.mywriterscircle.com**
International community of writers run by well-estab-
lished UK author Nick Daws. Another encouraging
respectful environment, with useful 'Review my work'
sections.

4   **www.freelancewritingtips.com**
Looks like a good one. Okay I'm one of the authors
— along with Craig McGinty — and we share our tips
and hints for a successful freelance career, with a dash
of humour. (We hope.)

5   **www.writethismoment.com**
Jobs board incorporating a beguiling range of jobs
across all writing disciplines. Small charge included.

6   **http://www.writelink.co.uk**
Well-supported lively, friendly site for new and aspiring
writers. Pays small fee for published articles.

Ghostwriting

What can you write about? Other people's stories can be a good source of income, especially if you are already used to spinning a good yarn as part of a magazine short story or feature.

Whose stories sell? Well of course celebrities already have the 'pull', or experts or business people might want to share their success. Then there are the so-called ordinary people who've been caught up in extraordinary circumstances. Take a trip to any major bookshop or even supermarket and you'll see the testimonies of overcoming tragedy or adversity lined up in the best sellers.

Writing for the stage & screen

Is your idea good enough?

The best thing you can bring is real life insight. Is the idea based on something unusual that happened to you, someone in your family, or someone you have interviewed? Contact TV producers to discuss your idea. Always remember not to take rejection personally. Develop a thick skin. It's a numbers game and always will be. As with any field of writing, you only need one "yes" to get you started.

Get past your great idea and make things happen! Most scripts that fail do so because the writer hasn't developed the action beyond the initial set-up. Screenplays may begin promisingly but then, about halfway in, the promise fizzles out. A bit like marriage you might think. You might be right. Don't let it happen to you!

Love your idea, nurture it, see it through and listen to where it wants to take you. Then hopefully, you won't hit a rocky patch.

Finding an agent

You have the *Writers' and Artists' Yearbook*. You have the Internet, you have 10 years' worth of back copies of your favourite writing magazines. So how are you going to find an agent? The answer is easier than you think. Ask other writers.

Get in touch with fellow freelance professionals, ask them what — and who — has worked for them.

DID YOU KNOW?

A is for apple

The original alphabet was developed by a Semitic people living in or near Egypt. They based it on the idea developed by the Egyptians, but used their own specific symbols. It was quickly adopted by their neighbours and relatives to the east and north, the Canaanites, the Hebrews, and the Phoenicians.

---

chapter summary:
Other writing

Remember:

- Give short stories a go.
- Look into non-fiction publishing.
- Make your synopsis compelling.
- If you don't ask you don't get.
- Find the right agent.

"If I'm trying to sleep, the ideas won't stop. If I'm trying to write, there appears a barren nothingness."

Carrie Latet

Commercial writing

chapter 7
Commercial writing

What do you mean by commercial writing?

Any writing work needed by a company. That could be copy for ads, brochures, websites, or whatever else there's a requirement for.

Believe you can do it

So long as you can write clearly and concisely, this work could be for you. The pay is good and it can be varied and interesting work – but there are downsides.

Be sure if it's for you

There's no doubt there's money to be made in this line of writing. Press releases, advertorials, marketing material copy, websites, brochures, sales letters – you name it, you can write it. But the question is, do you want to? Would you find it boring? Would it compromise your principles? Do you consider it beneath you?

The thing is, I have a mortgage to pay. Unless you are lucky enough to be able to pick and choose your writing projects, then commercial writing gigs might be at the top of your list.

Put yourself in the mind of the client

They want someone to supply a service. They want it done, quickly and efficiently. They want to see good results. They expect you to deliver. If you don't, they'll soon tell you in no uncertain terms.

They might not understand what you do or how you do it, but if they respect your skills they could become an excellent client.

A matter of ethics

If, alongside your commercial writing ventures, you want to maintain a good reputation as a journalist, then be careful how you go. You can't mix the two — any clash and you could be done for!

What do I mean? Well you absolutely can't contact the media on behalf of an organisation that has taken you on to do their PR. You are no longer objective, unless you make it abundantly clear that this is not the case.

A recent example from my own career was a story about a project being run by a local hospice. Instead of pitching it directly to a newspaper or specialist publication, I passed it to another freelancer. Why? Because my colleague Katie works on PR on behalf of that hospice, so my objectivity was lost. There was also the small matter of my company being paid by the charity to promote it, so it was just not right to then expect a commission from a paper.

Another example would be if a charity or organisation wanted you to publicise a new project, with the possibility of some interesting case studies. Fine, so long as you don't cross the line. You are acting as PR person here, not journalist, so don't think you can pitch an editor with details of your case studies. You have to find someone in the middle who is objective, impartial, and fair.

More on getting the work

I've detailed the joys of networking and marketing in the Do Your Own PR chapter. Always remember that no amount of advertising can guarantee you any work in this area. But the word of mouth that comes from doing a good job for someone who then recommends you to others, will be very beneficial.

With hand on heart I can say we haven't gone down the frankly terrifying route of cold calling either. While ringing an editor with an idea or sending out a pitch could be viewed as 'cold calling' in journalism, the thought of doing this for copy-writing work has no appeal, for a variety of reasons.

Get business cards printed and make them look as professional as possible.

On your cards don't just put name and contact details and basic job title – also list your services on the back. This sounds simple but is often overlooked. You could put:

- Journalism.
- Copywriting.
- Sub-editing.
- for online and corporate material. Or something similar.

There's plenty I could say about how to progress. Here's just a snippet:

- Always trust your instincts and take everything any business adviser tells you with a pinch of salt.

- Do not quote cheap because you are worried that customers will not want to pay more. You must value what you do and let them know that professional and well-written material is worth paying for.

- If you 'win' a customer on price, you could easily lose them on price. This is something I was warned about early on, and boy, did it come true.

- Always be aware that business owners can have very different approaches and expectations, not to mention ways of communicating, to an editor.

How clients will treat you

At all times remember they are the client — so remain professional. If changes are made to your copy, discuss this calmly. If someone is paying you for your expertise it can be frustrating, to say the least, if they then want to change your work back. You have to find the words to tell them firmly and respectfully why you have written something in a certain way. Put simply, it's based on your experience as a professional writer. If you don't feel you could manage to stay calm in such a situation then this work is definitely not for you.

When writing turns into public relations

Okay so you think you can write a press release, but can you persuade the media your client is worth reporting on? It's a tricky old game and one that you really should get more advice on. Know how to write a press release, what information is needed and who to send it to when, or whether a chat on the phone will suffice. Does that sound familiar? It should. Placing a story on behalf of a client can be pretty similar to successfully targeting a pitch.

PR: on the inside and the outside

PR is not just press releases. Communicating success both internally and externally is equally important, which is why good PR is very much at the heart and soul of every successful company, organisation, or, increasingly these days, celebrity.

UNDERSTAND WHAT PR CAN DO

You know what PR is don't you? You've heard of Max Clifford. You've seen him on the news every time a D-lister or a fading politician is caught with his pants down.

That's what PR is all about, right?

Wrong.

Worthwhile PR can reduce barriers to competition, open new markets, attract the best recruits and business partners, enhance access to funding and investors, and create a premium value for products and services, as well as protecting business in times of crisis.

Here's what leading agency Borkowski PR says good PR can lead to. I'm inclined to agree – I've quoted it enough times.

A party. You see a beautiful woman. You go over to her and say: "I'm brilliant in bed. Do you fancy spending the night with me?" That's advertising. You see another beautiful woman, and send your friend over to her. He says: "My friend is brilliant in bed. Do you fancy spending the night with him?" That's marketing. Then a third woman approaches you. She says: "I hear you're brilliant in bed. Do you fancy spending the night with me?" That's PR.

How not to do PR:

- Don't phone up a Sunday paper to ask: "Which day do your health pages come out?" It makes you look stupid. Incidentally, Sunday papers generally look for exclusives and won't simply publish your release three days after dailies have carried it.

- Don't send a release unless you have a good idea what kind of features/news the publication carries. You have to be prepared to actually read recent copies if you want to get it right.

- Don't try to be the journalist's best mate on the phone. They are usually busy and haven't got time for that.

- Don't send out completely untargeted press releases. Are you sure that *Mobile Phone Weekly* is really the place for your news of your new training course? ('It could be' isn't good enough!)

- Don't pester with repeat phone calls saying "are you going to use it?" One phone call asking this question is one too many. If the story is good enough, it will get in.

- Don't ask the journalist to dig out a piece they did ages ago to photocopy and send it to you. It's a really annoying and time consuming job and ensures they won't use anything else you send them in case they're asked to do the same again.

- Don't expect to take up loads of the journalist's time during a face-to-face meeting unless you honestly think your product or service could provide them with a significant story.

- If you are inviting the press to some sort of launch, be a bit generous and tell them what's on offer. It's a sad fact (but true) that journalists do respond to invites (more after-work events these days) if there is decent food and a couple of drinks on offer. It won't guarantee you coverage but you'll be remembered.

- If you are inviting the media to a photocall or local event and they tell you they hope to come along, don't ring up and moan when they don't. Guess what, they have other stuff to do!

- Don't ever complain that the media 'isn't getting behind' your product/service. That is not their job. Their job is to report the news.

Know what reporters think of you

Some may love you. Okay I lied.

On a scale of repulsiveness, somewhere amid dodgy door-to-door salesmen and super-smarmy telesales rip-off merchants, for many comes the not-so-humble PR practitioner. That's possibly on a par with journalist or writer, but probably below.

That's what the general public think, allegedly.

Even worse is the opinion of many journalists who reckon it's their job to tell the truth and yours to lie.

I have been guilty in the past of being ruder than most when nervous PRs have rung the newsdesk right on deadline to ask if I have received their press release about 'Tasty Treats for Spring'. But with a young family I have had to find other ways to make a living – and I have not looked back.

Six of the best

books for writers

1   *McNae's Essential Law for Journalists* by Tom Welsh, Walter Greenwood and David Banks (Oxford University Press)

Anyone who thinks legal matters won't affect them is kidding themselves. Start with getting to know about libel and contempt of court laws. Why? At worst you'll be in real trouble, at best you'll look a total idiot when an editor points out your oversight.

2   *The Renegade Writer: A Totally Unconventional Guide to Freelance Writing Success* by Linda Formichelli and Diana Burrell (Marion Street Press Inc)

This amazing book changed my life – yes it really is that good.

3   *The Freelance Handbook: How to make money and enjoy your life* by Andrew Crofts (Piatkus Books)

Much respected journalist and author Andrew Croft shows us how it can be done.

4   *The Well-Fed Writer: Financial Self-Sufficiency as a Freelance Writer in Six Months or Less* by Peter Bowerman (Fanove Publishing)

Basic steps to find the work – and bring home the bacon.

5 ***Writing for journalists* by Wynford Hicks, Sally Adams and Harriet Gilbert (Routledge)**
A classic by three highly experienced and trusted writing professionals – concentrating on the actual writing – well someone has to!

6 ***How to Write Articles for Newspapers and Magazines* by Dawn B Sova (Petersons)**
Well received tome on writing, recommended by freelance colleagues from Journobiz.com.

"Write your first draft with your heart. Re-write with your head.

from Finding Forrester

Don't be ripped off

Always always get an order form/contract signed up front. It's harsh but true that you cannot afford to do anything on trust. Some characters, unfortunately, will do anything to get out of paying. Establish stringent Terms and Conditions.

Know your competition

Find out what other writers charge for the work they do, and think about your own rates in comparison. Don't undervalue your services, experience, or skills.

Be realistic about where your work will come from

Have you heard of the 80/20 rule? You have now. The vast majority of your work (possibly 80 per cent) will come from a smaller proportion (say 20 per cent) of your clients.

You don't have to chase lots of customers but win more work from your existing ones. The salesmen will tell you it's far easier to convert an existing or previous client than it is to find new ones.

That means maximise income from each commercial client by going after all the work you can from them. Why be content with writing their marketing brochure when you could also be providing their newsletter and website copy?

Expect the unexpected

"There's nowt as queer as folk." I think this phrase was coined after dealings with commercial writing clients. Bless them. Of course most are wonderful to deal with (!) but the odd (sometimes very odd) one or two will cause you real problems.

They'll insist they know better than you and can write better than you. They'll pick fault with everything you do and then they'll string out paying. Get your money and run.

Nail the non-payers.

Every business – big or small – might fall victim to cashflow problems. If your clients have signed all the necessary paperwork and don't pay on time, find out why. There might be the rare occasion where you can let this pass, especially if they are up front with you.

But when the excuses continue, it's time to take action. Hold them at their word. They've signed your order form and had the work from you – it's time to pay up.

If you haven't been paid 30 days after invoicing, then send a statement. You might be entitled to interest on late payments. Check the Terms and Conditions they have agreed to.

You might also look into using a credit agency to return the money for you. These aren't baseball-wielding heavies – however much you wish they were. Instead they'll chase the debt on your behalf for a set fee or a proportion of the money owed.

The last resort might be the Small Claims Court. Follow it through and you can, and will, get your money back. In four years of trading, my company has been down this route three times – all in the first year.

That's because you develop a sixth sense – otherwise known as a bull**** detector. Make sure yours is switched on at all times! Seriously, go with your gut instinct from your first meeting with a potential client. If you don't like the look of them for whatever reason, there's no reason why you should feel compelled to do the work. There's plenty more out there.

chapter summary:
Commercial writing

Remember:

- Keep your options open with commercial writing work.
- Consider a move into public relations.
- Know how your clients will treat you – far differently from how editors will.
- Weigh up if it's really for you.
- How could it affect your writing for newspapers or magazines?

"If I fall asleep with a pen in my hand, don't remove it – I might be writing in my dreams.

Danzae Pace

Doing your own PR

chapter 8
Doing your own PR

Don't be shy, now or ever

If you think the world owes you a living as a freelance writer, then you are in the wrong job. You'll need tenacity and determination by the bucketful. You might have the most fantastic ideas in the world, but if you're not willing to chase customers, and that means editors, until you get a firm 'yes' or 'no', forget it. Knowing how and when to chase is a vital part of clinching that 'sale'.

Yes editors might sometimes come to you and ask you to do work for them, as will commercial clients, but the likelihood is that this won't be until you have a reputation as someone who can deliver. And even then you are up against many, many other writers who have been around for years, delivering their perfectly clean, legally sound, must-read copy, to deadline.

There's no point hiding your light under a bushel. You do really need to be broadcasting news of your skills, talents and experience to the world.

If the prospect of this is enough to make you want to run screaming for the hills then do yourself a favour and get out now.

Modesty isn't the best attribute when you have to make yourself stand out from the competition — in a good way.

Think of all the people you have to market yourself to, and get on with it.

Nurture your people skills

Don't hide behind your computer keyboard. Get out there, meet people, get yourself known in the right circles, attend the right events, get in touch with contacts, potential clients, and inter-viewees, even the dreaded PR people. Go and have a coffee with them, or even treat them to lunch.

Join influential groups according to your specialism

Writers can find the likes of The Guild of Health Writers, travel writers' groups and their local NUJ branch or media networking groups pretty useful. Not only can they help ease the isolation a freelance can feel, but they can also have some wonderful guests, giving you the opportunity to meet senior people in your chosen field. That's got to be a good thing, so long as you're not feeling too nervous.

Get webwise

Set up a website to showcase your work. This needn't be expen-sive. There are several free systems that allow you to present a homepage and portfolio. Talk to friends and colleagues about which systems work for them and go with something they advise you can trust. Make sure your contact details are prominent. But don't assume a website will sell your work for you. Work hard to promote it.

Point editors to your cuttings on there at the end of pitches, take part in groups and forums where you'll have the opportunity to have a signature with your website address on it, link out as much as possible to interesting news sites, to your latest piece of work and to freelance colleagues to name but a few. Here's hoping they'll consider doing the same in return — which is all grist to the mill for search engines' mysterious search powers.

Ask yourself: What's in a name?

Who could've guessed that a firm named after someone who's inexperienced in the bedroom department would really 'fly', or that a phone firm with a colour as its 'brand' could be quite so successful? Getting your name right or wrong can mean make or break for the fledgling entrepreneur — and yes, have you twigged yet that I mean you?

Be strong from the start

Making people remember you because of a strong name is a boost from Day One in business. Also remember that all that you do as a company should reflect the same 'brand'. Find a name that isn't already out there. Check through listings at Companies House to make sure your great idea isn't already taken. Check that the domain name isn't already registered. Register the name as a trademark to ensure nobody else uses it.

Six of the best

where can you find story ideas?

1 **Contacts nurtured in various walks of life ...**
The gift of the gab can go a long way. Talk to people, find their stories, look after them.

2 **From your own life – your family and your friends ...**
Why not? Start with your nearest and dearest.

3 **Charities and community organisations ...**
Ask about any awareness campaigns, achievements or people they have helped, who'd like to tell their story.

4 **Businesses ...**
Any genuine innovations or discussions of current issues in a given field might be useful – but don't fall into the trap of letting them think you are doing their PR.

5 **Down the pub ...**
Speaks for itself. I hope.

6 **www.holdthefrontpage.co.uk ...**
A site for UK regional journalists, also has a 'story ideas' section.

There's nothing wrong with your own name you know!

I changed to Passionate Media because there are another million Linda Joneses out there. But beware, in this element you might like to do as I say, not do as I do. Passionate Media might sound okay to the business down the road that wants some PR. It might also "fit" with women's magazines. But does it always go down well with the switchboard? Well no it doesn't actually, especially when they think we are call girls. And the fine upstanding journalists on the more high-minded journals do also seem a bit befuddled by it!

Top tips for finding a name that's right for you:

- Relate your choice of name in some way to you, your story, or what your company is about. It sounds a bit weak if you say "I just liked the name"!

- If marketing in directories (online or even Yellow Pages) is going to be an important part of your marketing, don't call your company something beginning with Z. Your customers will have got bored and called one of your competitors before they get to you.

- If Internet marketing and a web presence is going to be very important to you ensure that your name is not too long or too easy to get wrong.

- Consider alliteration to make your name memorable.

- Save cash by thinking things through.

PR consultant Shirley Mann of Harvest PR (**www.harvestpr.net**) says this name expressed a deep felt commitment to the environment without being too reminiscent of sandals and corduroy!

She also raises an important point often considered by smaller businesses.

"I didn't want my name to be part of the company, because I wanted it to be bigger than just one person. The logo was the next thing. Again, I wanted to make sure that it said something so we opted for a contemporary design while still reflecting the core values of the company.

"Firms can spend millions on a logo. I have a friend who does graphics from home but works to such a high standard, she is used by international firms. By just suggesting to her the base from which we wanted to start, she came up with exactly what I wanted for a very reasonable cost. If firms think through their own ideas before going to the graphic designers, they could save themselves a great deal of money."

Shirley also advises:

- Fashionable names are dangerous – remember Mavis once was a very popular girls' name.
- If you want to have kudos, you'll need to have something that suggests professionalism, class, and expertise.
- A name can result in publicity in itself – hopefully of the right sort!

To editors…

Yes sending a pitch they can't turn down is the most fail-safe way of winning work from a hard-pressed editor. But think how much more likely they are to remember you if you have taken the time to keep in touch after a previous commission, or have met them at a networking do, or even been out for lunch with them. It does happen you know!

IF AT FIRST YOU DON'T SUCCEED
Send regular pitches to a section you know commissions freelance work, and if they are good enough, one day you will crack it. Don't give up. How you react when you don't get the work as well as when you do is what marks you out as a professional.

There's a fine line...

Don't be a nuisance. Editors are busy people. Don't pester. How quickly can they realistically be expected to come back to you? Remember at all times they never actually asked you to get in touch. (Well unless of course they did, but then you should be quids-in anyway.)

So when the time is right, pick up that phone

Of course what you don't do, as a complete newbie, is to ring every editor you'd be writing for in your dreams. Instead, be realistic – are they likely to have the time or want to meet you? Why should they? When could they meet you, what are their deadlines, and what sort of ideas do they want to see?

Meeting an editor for coffee might be one of the most nerve-wracking experiences you care to wind yourself up about, but it's also one of the most worthwhile.

Don't forget about job ads

Okay so these are mainly for staff jobs. But tucked away in the same ad may also be a call-out for freelance contributors. Even if there isn't such an appeal, you have nothing to lose with a polite enquiry as to whether there might be any opportunities.

There is also now a wealth of resources online that advertise freelance positions. I'd say the best in the UK would be **www.journalism.co.uk** as most others seem to be taken up with full-time positions. Check every Monday. Then there's **www.writethismoment.com** which has an impressive array of opportunities from all disciplines, rather than just journalism.

There's no better advert than word of mouth

If you are ever going away on holiday or languishing in your sickbed when a commission comes through, don't promise to deliver then fail. Why not recommend a fellow freelance instead? Wouldn't you quite reasonably hope that they might return the favour one day?

Are online directories out of line?

No, they're not. Get yourself listed. The NUJ has a directory which allows members to advertise for a small sum, the price of which should take you less than an hour to earn. Other websites including **www.journalism.co.uk**, **www.holdthefrontpage.co.uk** and **www.journobiz.com** also have their own lists. I've found work through all of them.

Use your space on the list well

Don't just say you are a freelance journalist who can deliver copy on time. Some editors might just take that for granted. Like a plumber saying they're friendly and professional, wouldn't you sort of take for granted the fact you can write? What about spelling out your experience and expertise? List some of your commissions and explain what makes you different. We're back to banishing modesty again!

To commercial clients…

Network, network, network.

Network as much as you can. Find out about groups for local businesses, or national groups covering your interests. Go along to the meetings. It will pay off. If you find the people strange (and you might) then join another group – or start your own.

To network or not to network at breakfast time?

If you're getting up for a 9am start anyway, then maybe setting the alarm 90 minutes earlier isn't too terrible, especially as it means you'll beat the rush-hour traffic into the town or city centre. And for many, it's preferable to having to attend a meeting at the end of the day, when all you want to do is get home. On the other hand, if you have a young family, leaving the house so early could be problematic. For example, if your children go to nursery or school, these don't open 'til after you need to be at the breakfast meeting.

How can a creative company/ start-up benefit?

I have often been the only person there who does journalism and/or PR. The interest, when you say what you do, is palpable. For start-ups, breakfast networking clubs are a way of marketing yourself reasonably cheaply without resorting to expensive advertising/marketing/PR campaigns. You are effectively buying into a captive audience which is receptive to the idea of giving you business or passing your details on to other contacts.

Six of the best
questions to ask before seeking a career in freelance writing

1   **Can I afford it?**
What are my outgoings and how am I going to cover them?

2   **How do I cope with rejection?**
Don't let it get you down. Pick yourself up and start all over again.

3   **How nervous am I?**
Not too nervous to ring an editor or chase for money, I hope.

4   **What makes me so special?**
Why should editors choose my work over that of a million other wannabe contributors?

5   **How's my grammar?**
Very important one this. Sort it out!

6   **Erm, what can I write about, and who for?**
Now there's a question! Be realistic, else you'll get nowhere, fast.

Consider NOT joining

Yes you read that right. Some people will tell you all of these groups are far too expensive. As well as a joining fee of hundreds of pounds, you have to pay for each breakfast, which ranges from £7 to £10.

You can get yourself invited as a guest to one club, which invariably leads to your being invited as a guest by someone else to a different organisation. That's enough for some to get the contacts you need for a kick-start. But you must be careful of gaining yourself a reputation as a fly by night.

Ask yourself: is this group of people for you?

These groups essentially run on a 'you scratch my back and I'll scratch yours' type principle. Either get used to that and get on with it, or bail out before it all becomes too unbearable.

Start your own group

If you can't make a meeting because of the time or you don't click with the people there, then rest assured others will feel exactly the same way. You just have to find them! And how do you do that? Well as you are in the communications business, you might want to think about letting people know the opportunity is there. Publicise the new group through your local or specialist press, on your website, and through word of mouth.

Think of networking like dating. You have to kiss a lot of frogs, before you find your match. Give networking a chance. Love at first sight really doesn't happen that often.

Advertising your services

There are several roads you could go down. Do you want to specialise or do you want to keep all options open? Do you have the time and energy to go and network, and what's your view on mailshots, postcard campaigns, and cold calling?

Don't think promotion = advertising

So where should you advertise? Possibly nowhere. There's nothing to beat word of mouth, which comes from doing a good job for someone, who is then willing to recommend you on.

Join forces for more pitching power!

Contact local design, marketing, PR and printing companies to discuss recommending your services to anyone wanting a website, brochure, media campaign, or proof-reader. They wouldn't take a chance with the more technical part, so convince them of the value of commissioning a writer to do the writing. Put like that it sounds so simple, but it can be quite a struggle. Persevere; it will pay off in the end.

Contact not for profit, local authority and charitable organisations

Find out what writing they have to do (usually a mountain of it) and offer your services — once you've established there is a budget of course. But this is where personally I'd say a little bit of favour-doing can pay off in the long-run — so long as you go in with your eyes open and make the most of other opportunities this brings you.

To people you could be writing about ...

E-sy does it

Start your own e-newsletter and send it out to your contact list. The more people who know about you and what you do, the more likely they are to approach you with ideas.

Keep in touch

If you're having a quiet time – or even if you're not – put in some phone calls or emails to your contacts. Ask them if they have 'any news' and you're bound to come up with some story ideas, even if they don't recognise what they tell you as such.

Be prepared to stand out from the crowd

I had some postcards printed with the image of a young woman jumping joyfully though the air, against a clear blue sky. I gave it the slogan "we think you're amazing" and dropped off copies with beauty salons, hairdressers, laundrettes and shops. The clutch of inspirational women's magazine stories that it brought in were well worth it.

Get to know PR people

Yes it has to be done. Don't get too matey though – this is an easy trap to fall into. Some people say that it's a journalist's job to tell the truth and a PR agent's to hide it. I wouldn't go that far – not all journalists are paragons of virtue, after all. But remember at all times that a PR agent's remit is to promote their client, not to get you what you see as the best story they can.

Sign up to Response Source for regular press releases and updates of what's going on in your chosen field. Include the PR companies in your e-newsletters and get on as many mailing lists as you can.

Remain cool, polite and professional at all times, even if you feel like banging your head on the table when your questions just aren't being answered. Why? Well because you want them to share their next "exclusive" with you.

Alternatively, you could go with the banging your head on the table option. PRs aren't always best known for their understanding of what writers need.

To the media as an expert...

Cultivate your blog (see Chapter Four), get yourself listed on **www.expertsources.co.uk** for a small fee, and comment on hot topics of the day in your chosen field. Write letters to editors. Unleash your inner Victor Meldrew and the enquiries should start coming in.

DID YOU KNOW?

Pen and paper

The origins of the pen date back to ancient Egypt where scribes dipped pointed reeds into pigments with which to write upon papyrus. Over the millennia, the reed was eventually replaced by a sharpened quill, which was supplanted, in turn, by the development in the early 1800s of the metal nib (penpoint). Paper was invented by the Chinese 2000 years ago. Although humans had used other flat substances upon which to write – clay tablets, hide parchment, and papyrus, from which we get the word paper – none of these are truly paper. Paper is made of a layer of felt of randomly oriented plant fibres.

---

chapter summary:
Doing your own PR

Remember:

- Don't hide behind your keyboard thinking work will come to you – get out there and find it.
- Network as much as you can.
- Keep up to date with your specialism.
- Nurture your contacts.
- Form strategic alliances with promising looking organisations.

Checklist: **Newspaper article**

Tick off all of the following to make sure your newspaper article cuts the mustard:

- [ ] **Who:** Have you checked how to spell everyone's names? Be sure to put "all names correct" in a note at the end of your copy.

- [ ] **Find out:** Age; address; job; contact details; relationship with other people and birthday (will they be another year older by the time the piece comes out?) Make sure the people interviewed are relevant to the readership of the publication.

- [ ] **What:** Do you understand exactly what has happened, or is going to happen and why? Can you explain this clearly and succinctly? Remember there's no such thing as a stupid question. If they have to read any part of it twice, then you've failed.

- [ ] **When:** Check all your dates are correct before you submit. Often the style of the publication may be to include the day of the week, the date and the month.

- [ ] **Why and how:** Often the best part of the story! Answer any questions that arise – half the story is no good. Put yourself in the readers' position again and ask away!

- [ ] **Where:** A local paper might want a street name, but not a more widely read publication.

- [ ] **Use the right style:** Check out current or past editions of the publication you're writing for to make sure you are on the right track.

☐ **Mind your language:** Don't use six words to say something you could in one. Avoid jargon and just keep it simple.

☐ **A capital offence:** Legalese may demand every second word be capped up, but not a newspaper.

☐ **A question of spelling and grammar:** One "definately" is one too many. The same goes for womens, banana's or 1970's.

☐ **How's your intro?** Any more than 30 words and it could be a no-no. Make your readers read on.

☐ **Limit sentences per paragraph:** Three might be too many.

☐ **Let your fingers do the talking:** Make your copy come alive: use a mix of direct and indirect speech. Quotes should be exciting, interesting and thought-provoking. Don't get carried away with the exclamation marks or descriptive verbs.

☐ **Spellcheck again and again:** Just in case you've inadvertently changed some words to something quite different. It might be hilarious, but the telling off you get if the first time it's spotted is in the paper, won't be.

☐ **Play fair:** Unless it's an opinion piece, make sure you have given any opposing viewpoints a balanced, unbiased slice of the action. And even if it is an opinion piece, still play fair! Make sure nothing you have written is offensive or potentially libellous. If you're not sure what this means, you're not ready to start.

☐ **Above all:** Meet requirements. Follow your brief to the letter – wordcount and deadline haven't been put there for fun. Get them wrong and there may not be a next time.

Checklist: **Magazine article**

Tick off all of the following to make sure your magazine article will hit the mark:

☐ **Who:** Get the basics right. Have you checked how to spell everyone's names? Be sure to put "all names correct" in a note at the end of your copy. Do you understand their relationship to everyone else in the piece?

☐ **Find out:** Age; address; job; contact details; relationship with other people and birthday (will they be another year older by the time the piece comes out?).

Learn about right to reply and where it's needed. Find relevant expert comment if it's needed: use a bonafide expert – not just someone attempting to publicise their own work.

☐ **What:** Do you understand exactly what has happened, or is going to happen and why? Can you explain this clearly and succinctly? Remember there's no such thing as a stupid question. If they have to read any part of it twice, then you've failed.

☐ **When:** Know your lead-in times. It's no good pitching a Christmas article in November or a Valentine's piece in February. Monthly magazines plan for months ahead and even weekly magazines can have a long wait.

Look at the way your story pans out – if you are telling a personal story, then start at the beginning and tell it chronologically rather than using an intro that attempts to pack in all the facts.

☐ **Check all your dates are correct before you submit:** Often the style of the publication might be to include the day of the week, the date and the month.

☐ **Know what's happening with pictures:** Is the magazine taking their own? Do they need "collects"? (Family album pictures or those submitted by an interviewee.)

☐ **Tell the story:** Include as much detail and colour as you can, without waffling on. Use short sentences that help the reader along. Introduce dialogue where necessary and keep the flow.

☐ **Where:** They may not care as much as a paper, but it's still important to get locations right. Sometimes even the sub editors might get it wrong, so give them all the help you can – by getting it right in the first place.

☐ **How's your intro?** Be as creative as you like – but still hook the reader in.

☐ **Spellcheck again and again:** Just in case you've inadvertently changed some words to something quite different. It can happen you know and when it does it might be hilarious, but the telling off you get if the first time it's spotted is in the magazine, won't be.

☐ **Above all:** Meet requirements. Follow your brief to the letter – wordcount and deadline haven't been put there for fun. Get them wrong and there might not be a next time.

Checklist: **Blog post**

Tick off all of the following to make sure your blog post is as attractive as it can be:

- [ ] **The heading:** Make it easy to find on the major search engines. Be as jokey as you like but at least mention what you're writing about.

- [ ] **Link, then link some more:** Link to outside sites that interest you and are mentioned in your piece, but also link to previous posts on you own blog – they're a long time in your archive and it will increase time spent on your site if your readers have more of a mooch around. Include related post links with your latest piece.

  But don't make links what pro-blogger Craig McGinty calls "speed bumps" – so many links they just get in your way.

- [ ] **Be topical:** Write about that burning issue, today, not next week! The conversation will have moved on.

- [ ] **Keep it short, simple and if at all possible ... entertaining:** Who's going to come back to a blog that is as dull as ditchwater?

- [ ] **Use multiple categories:** Increase the chances of your reader finding your post in the future by including it in your blog's different categories.

- [ ] **Use Technorati tags:** These will show you who else is discussing the same stuff. Keep up with the conversation. Drop by at their blogs too and leave a comment, who knows they might come and check you out too.

☐ **Enable comments and trackbacks:** It's good manners to listen to your readers – and to respond to them too. It might be time-consuming, but you want to interact, don't you? Else what's the point?

☐ **Include an excerpt:** For anyone keeping up with your blog through a feed as opposed to clicking on to the homepage.

☐ **Stick to the same style:** Be consistent. Find your style for names, dates etc and stick to it. Anything else looks sloppy.

☐ **Don't overlook images – but be aware of copyright:** Use your own pictures, request publicity shots or ask permission. You wouldn't want someone to rip off your words, so don't rip off other people's images.

☐ **Break up longer articles in to shorter posts:** Extend your post to get more page impressions.

☐ **Also:** Read through all the pointers in the newspaper article checklist and make sure you get to grips with most of that too – especially understanding libel!

Recommended reading

Essential English: For Journalists, Editors and Writers
by Harold Evans (Pimlico)
ISBN-13: 978-0712664479

*From Pitch to Publication: Everything You
Need to Know to Get Your Novel Published*
by Carole Blake (Pan Books)
ISBN-13: 978-0333714355

How to Get Published and Make a Lot of Money
by Susan Blake (Piatkus Books)
ISBN-13: 978-0749919467

*The Novelist's Guide: Powerful Techniques
for Creating Character, Dialogue and Plot*
by Margaret Geraghty (Piatkus Books)
ISBN-13: 978-0749916534

Writers' and Artists' Yearbook 2007
(A&C Black Publishers Ltd.)
ISBN-13: 978-0713677126

The Writer's Handbook 2007
by Barry Turner (MacMillan)
ISBN-13: 978-1405049375

On Writing
by Stephen King (New English Library Ltd)
ISBN-13: 978-0340820469

*The Creative Writing Coursebook: Forty Authors
Share Advice and Exercises for Fiction and Poetry*
by Andrew Moreton & Julia Bell (Pan Books)
ISBN-13: 978-0333782255

The Complete Idiot's Guide to Writing a Novel
by Tom Monteleone (Alpha Books)
ISBN-13: 978-1592571727

McNae's Essential Law for Journalists
by Tom Welsh, Walter Greenwood and David Banks
(Oxford University Press)
ISBN-13: 978-0199284184

*The Renegade Writer: A Totally Unconventional Guide
to Freelance Writing Success*
by Linda Formichelli and Diana Burrell (Marion Street Press Inc)
ISBN-13: 978-1933338002

*The Freelance Handbook:
How to make money and enjoy your life*
by Andrew Crofts (Piatkus Books)
ISBN-13: 978-0749923099

*The Well-Fed Writer: Financial Self-Sufficiency
as a Freelance Writer in Six Months or Less*
by Peter Bowerman (Fanove Publishing)
ISBN-13: 978-0967059846

Writing for journalists
by Wynford Hicks, Sally Adams and Harriet Gilbert (Routledge)
ISBN-13: 978-0415184458

How to Write Articles for Newspapers and Magazines
by Dawn B Sova (Petersons)
ISBN-13: 978-0768910797

Useful addresses

HM REVENUE & CUSTOMS

www.hmrc.gov.uk

Companies House:
Tel: 0870 33 33 636 or
02920 381245

Email: enquiries@
companies-house.gov.uk
**www.companieshouse.
gov.uk**

Main Office:
Companies House
Crown Way
Maindy
Cardiff CF14 3UZ

HM TREASURY

The Correspondence &
Enquiry Unit
2/W1 HM Treasury
1 Horse Guards Road
London SW1A 2HQ

Tel 020 7270 4558
Fax 020 7270 4861

www.hm-treasury.gov.uk

BUSINESS REFERRAL EXCHANGE (BRE)

18 Pine Grove,
Brookmans Park
Hertfordshire AL9 7BS

Tel: 01707 644822
Fax: 01707 663847

Email: enquiries@brenet.co.uk
www.brenet.co.uk

CHAMBERS OF COMMERCE

The British Chambers of
Commerce
65 Petty France
London SW1H 9EU

Tel: 020 7654 5800
Fax: 020 7654 5819

Email:
info@britishchambers.org.uk
www.chamberonline.co.uk

*For business services
enquiries contact:*

The British Chambers of
Commerce
4 Westwood House,
Westwood Business Park
Coventry CV4 8HS

Tel: 024 7669 4484
Fax: 024 7669 5844

BUSINESS LINK

Tel: 0845 600 9 006
www.businesslink.gov.uk

BNI

Business Network
International plc
BNI House
Church Street
Rickmansworth WD3 1BS

Office: 01923-891-999
Fax: 01923-891-998

Email: bniuk@eurobni.com
www.bni-europe.com

THE WOMEN'S NETWORKING COMPANY

**www.thewomens
networkingcompany.com**

Further support and help for
women can be found at the
following websites:

**www.motheratwork.co.uk
www.homeworking.com
www.enterprisingwoman.
co.uk
www.everywoman.co.uk**

WINGS

Women's independent
networking groups (Midlands)

www.wings.uk.net

NCTJ TRAINING LTD

The New Granary
Station Road
Newport, Saffron Walden
Essex CB11 3PL

Tel: 01799 544014
Fax: 01799 544015

Email: info@nctj.com
www.nctj.com

THE JOURNALISM DIVERSITY FUND

NCTJ Training Ltd
The New Granary
Station Road
Newport, Saffron Walden
Essex CB11 3PL

Tel: 01799 544014
Fax: 01799 544015

E-mail: journalismdiversity-
fund@fsmail.net
**www.journalismdiversity
fund.com**

NUJ – NATIONAL UNION OF JOURNALISTS

Headland House
308-312 Gray's Inn Road
London WC1X 8DP

Tel: 020 7278 7916
Fax: 020 7837 8143

Email: info@nuj.org.uk
www.nuj.org.uk

CHARTERED INSTITUTE OF PUBLIC RELATIONS

CIPR Public Relations Centre
32 St. James's Square
London SW1Y 4JR

Tel: 020 7766 3333
Fax: 020 7766 3344

Email: info@cipr.co.uk
www.ipr.org.uk

THE CHARTERED INSTITUTE OF JOURNALISTS

2 Dock Offices
Surrey Quays Road
LONDON SE16 2XU

Tel: 020 7252 1187
Fax: 020 7232 2302

Email: memberservices@cioj.co.uk
www.cioj.co.uk

SOCIETY FOR PROOFREADERS AND EDITORS

www.sfep.org.uk

SOCIETY OF EDITORS

University Centre
Granta Place
Mill Lane
Cambridge CB2 1RU

Tel: 01223 304080
Fax: 01223 304090

www.societyofeditors.co.uk

THE AUTHORS' LICENSING AND COLLECTING SOCIETY

ALCS Ltd
The Writers' House
13 Haydon Street
London EC3N 1DB

Tel: 020 7264 5700
Fax: 020 7264 5755

Email: alcs@alcs.co.uk
www.alcs.co.uk

THE MEDIA SOCIETY

**www.themediasociety.
co.uk**

THE NEWSPAPER SOCIETY

St. Andrew's House
18-20 St. Andrew Street
London EC4A 3AY

Tel: 020 7632 7400
Fax: 020 7632 7401

Email:
ns@newspapersoc.org.uk
www.newspapersoc.org.uk

PRESS COMPLAINTS COMMISSION

Halton House
20/23 Holborn
London EC1N 2JD

www.pcc.org.uk

FURTHER READING

Press Gazette
www.pressgazette.co.uk

Writers' News & Writing
magazine
www.writersnews.co.uk

The New Writer
www.thenewwriter.com

Index

Disclaimer
The websites, services and resources listed in this book have not paid for their entries – they are included as a guideline only and the author/publisher does not endorse their products or services.

Index – Six of the Best

Acknowledgments

Thanks to Jan Murray and Ed Miller from JournoBiz for their tireless work to connect journalists in a calm and welcoming environment and giving me the opportunity to find so many more friends, great advice and much-valued work. Thanks to everyone else at JournoBiz for their continued friendship.

Thanks to my friends and colleagues at Passionate Media.

Much love and appreciation go to blogging superstar Craig McGinty and big hugs and kisses go to Neil, Emily and Melissa for always being there and letting me get on with things.

Thanks also to Kelly Rose Bradford for her support in my journey into writing fiction and for her encouragement that made this possible in the first place.

Thanks to Nick Daws for inspiring a more "rounded" writing career when all I feared I was fit to write about was local news, and thanks to Andrew Crofts for the sound knowledge he imparted to boost my ghostwriting prospects.

'The Greatest Tips in the World' books

Baby & Toddler Tips
by Vicky Burford
ISBN 978-1-905151-70-7

Barbeque Tips
by Raymond van Rijk
ISBN 978-1-905151-68-4

Cat Tips by Joe Inglis
ISBN 978-1-905151-66-0

Cookery Tips
by Peter Osborne
ISBN 978-1-905151-64-6

Cricketing Tips
by R. Rotherham & G. Clifford
ISBN 978-1-905151-18-9

DIY Tips
by Chris Jones & Brian Lee
ISBN 978-1-905151-62-2

Dog Tips by Joe Inglis
ISBN 978-1-905151-67-7

Etiquette & Dining Tips
by Prof. R. Rotherham
ISBN 978-1-905151-21-9

Freelance Writing Tips
by Linda Jones
ISBN 978-1-905151-17-2

Gardening Tips
by Steve Brookes
ISBN 978-1-905151-60-8

Genealogy Tips
by M. Vincent-Northam
ISBN 978-1-905151-72-1

Golfing Tips
by John Cook
ISBN 978-1-905151-63-9

Horse & Pony Tips
by Joanne Bednall
ISBN 978-1-905151-19-6

Household Tips
by Vicky Burford
ISBN 978-1-905151-61-5

Personal Success Tips
by Brian Larcher
ISBN 978-1-905151-71-4

Podcasting Tips
by Malcolm Boyden
ISBN 978-1-905151-75-2

Property Developing Tips
by F. Morgan & P Morgan
ISBN 978-1-905151-69-1

Retirement Tips
by Tony Rossiter
ISBN 978-1-905151-28-8

Sex Tips
by Julie Peasgood
ISBN 978-1-905151-74-5

Travel Tips
by Simon Worsfold
ISBN 978-1-905151-73-8

Yoga Tips
by D. Gellineau & D. Robson
ISBN 978-1-905151-65-3

Pet Recipe books

The Greatest Feline Feasts in the World by Joe Inglis
ISBN 978-1-905151-50-9

The Greatest Doggie Dinners in the World by Joe Inglis
ISBN 978-1-905151-51-6

'The Greatest in the World' DVDs

The Greatest in the World – Gardening Tips
presented by Steve Brookes

The Greatest in the World – Yoga Tips
presented by David Gellineau and David Robson

The Greatest in the World – Cat & Kitten Tips
presented by Joe Inglis

The Greatest in the World – Dog & Puppy Tips
presented by Joe Inglis

For more information about currently available
and forthcoming book and DVD titles please visit:

www.thegreatestintheworld.com

or write to:

The Greatest in the World Ltd
PO Box 3182
Stratford-upon-Avon
Warwickshire CV37 7XW
United Kingdom
Tel / Fax: +44(0)1789 299616
Email: info@thegreatestintheworld.com

The author

From detailing the horror of receiving big pants for Christmas in *Bella* to reporting on the heinous crimes of Fred West for regional media, Linda's career has spanned nearly two decades and seen work published in dozens of publications.

A former news editor on the *Wolverhampton Express & Star* and the *Worcester Evening News*, she has also worked as a senior reporter at several regional newspapers. She now writes on subjects including technology, parenting and journalism for titles including *The Guardian* and *Press Gazette*. Publications she has edited include *Tamba's Twins, Triplets & More* magazine and the *St Petersburg Press* in Russia.

Her company Passionate Media, founded in 2003, supplies commercial writing services for national and local clients. Linda is a co-editor of the **www.freelancewritingtips.com** website.